THE URBAN KITCHEN GARDENER

GROWING & COOKING IN THE CITY

TOM MOGGACH

Kyle Books

KEY

Which parts of
the plant are
good to eat

How much direct
sunlight the plant
needs

Will grow in
semi-shady
spots

Will tolerate a
small amount
of shade

Thrives best
in full sunlight

How well-suited
the plant is
to growing in
pots and other
containers

1/5   2/5   3/5   4/5   5/5

Not suitable
for container
growing

Ideal for
container
growing

The publishers have made every effort to contact all copyright holders for permissions. Those we have been unable to reach are invited to contact us so that a full acknowledgment may be given.

CONTENTS

To help with navigation, this book groups plants into the categories above. Note, however, that the reality is more complex — and appetising. The leaves of beetroot, carrots, nasturtiums, radishes and most herbs are also terrific in salads, for example. Many of the plants also produce edible flowers. The key with each plant entry will help to explain which parts you can eat.

INTRODUCTION

Growing food is different in the city. Life is faster and space is tight. We're spoilt for choice, with lots to juggle. So we garden to bring balance and a natural joy to our days, raising plants that offer us terrific ingredients to eat.

In this book, you will find my top edible plants for the urban gardener. They offer tasty harvests from compact urban plots, and many are tricky to buy. I also cover honey and eggs, plus ideas for green and low-cost gardening, preserving your harvest, saving seed and much more.

All my advice is rooted firmly in practical realities — what works, and is worth the effort. I will show you how to eat well from your plot, whatever its size. I was born in the city, and urban gardening is what I know. I now help people to grow food on balconies, window ledges, rooftops, patios, allotments, and in back gardens and community plots. I'm a qualified teacher, so schools are my particular favourites.

I love to cook and worked in restaurants before becoming a food journalist. So I'm fascinated by the diverse ethnic flavours of our cities and how best to show off our harvest in the kitchen.

We're actually the lucky ones, gardening in an urban environment. Smaller spaces help us to focus. Why bother growing the staples? We're blessed with all manner of food shops and restaurants. Self-sufficiency is not on our menu, and sounds rather dull to me. Baking potatoes, for example, are dirt cheap, so sink low on the list. Save your space for chillies and strawberries, or shiso and sorrel – hard-to-buy herbs that are easy to grow.

Cities also provide a microclimate, with a few precious degrees of extra heat and shelter from extremes of weather. It's possible to bend the normal rules of gardening – stretching the season, escaping hard frosts and experimenting with less traditional crops.

Growing edible plants also has other juicy benefits. A huge perk is that we can eat plants at any stage in their life cycle, which is impossible with shop-bought produce. We can spice up our cooking with coriander leaf, for example, or wait for the delicious white flowers and green seeds – a fantastic ingredient that you cannot buy. Or relish sweet baby carrots pulled straight from the earth.

We can also save some cash, especially by growing high-value crops such as salad leaves or herbs. We reduce household costs, too, by picking exactly the amount we need, cutting down on waste and half-used packets.

On the other hand, what price can you put on simple pleasures? One perfectly ripe strawberry, eaten warm from the sun, offers more happiness than a dozen stashed for days in the fridge.

On a deeper level, I reckon that raising plants helps us to feel more happy and satisfied. Growing food chimes with our ancient DNA. We are here now because our ancestors tilled the land.

Gardening is a wonderful antidote to the buzz of city life. It wakes up the senses and gets us outdoors. It is, in a memorable phrase, 'playtime for adults', and teaches us how to live with a lighter touch, wasting less and enjoying more.

Through gardening, I've learnt to open my eyes to the world outside my windows. I look up when I walk the streets and tune in to the beauty of the natural world, the nuances of weather and seasons.

Just one pot on the windowsill will make you feel better. It's a simple, uncomplicated relationship, unlike all others. So get growing.

URBAN PLOTS

Squashed for space, urban growers rely on ingenuity and creativity to grow plants wherever we can. We create beautiful plots in unlikely spots, bringing life to where previously there was little.

That's why I love cycling around the city, spotting the tell-tale foliage of a secret roof garden or trundling past a guerrilla veg patch. I've visited gardens in disused railway sidings, on the top of smart office blocks and even on floating canal barges.

In the sections below, I spell out my top tips for successful gardening in typical urban locations: windowsills, rooftops, balconies, patios, community gardens and allotments. But first it's worth noting some general principles for assessing the growing potential of any site.

Understanding your plot

The foundation of good gardening is to understand your growing space – its sunny spots, dark corners and draughty bits, as this will determine where and what to plant.

On most city plots, the sun slides behind buildings for a chunk of each day, shielding the direct light. In contrast, most rural plots are more open and unobstructed.

First, work out the how much light the plot enjoys, both from direct sun and indirect light. Choose a day with clear skies, when you are staying at home. Then sketch a bird's-eye view of your growing space and systematically note the sun's movement every few hours. Use a compass, if needed, to get to grips with how the sun moves across the sky.

Over time, you can also gauge how the light levels change through the seasons. In winter, for example, the sun lies lower in the sky, so a previously bright spot may become chilly and shaded.

Gaps between buildings will channel and strengthen the wind, which may damage or chill your plants. On a blustery day, check which areas are exposed or sheltered. Identify hot and cooler spots, perhaps using a simple garden thermometer to help.

All this information will inform your next steps. Are your plants in the right position? Chillies, for example, need full sun; leafy salads will tolerate a touch of shade. The 'sun' rating for individual plants in the book will help with further guidance.

Consider if you can expand your growing space. Extra levels or shelves will boost capacity. You could grow in tiers, or vertically, using trellis and other tricks. For instance, I've just drilled vine eyes along one wall on my balcony to attach string for climbing beans. Peas, mouse melons and squashes are examples of other edible climbers.

Finally, a note on pollution. I sometimes meet people who are concerned about the effect on their crops of vehicle exhaust fumes and other pollutants in the urban environment. Scientific research has shown that there is no cause for concern in ground-level plots that are three metres or more away from a main road. Balconies and other raised plots have the advantage of further distance. If in doubt, wash produce before eating and take solace in the fact that any possible increase in particles of lead, platinum and other pollutants are so minute that they pose no risk to human health.

Clockwise from top left:
Balcony growing in Paris;
balcony in London;
community garden in New York;
fire escape in New York

Indoor windowsills

Temperatures are typically higher and more stable indoors. Windowsills therefore offer extra warmth and protection so are particularly useful for raising seedlings and tender plants.

A sunny windowsill, for example, is ideal for sun-lovers such as chillies, tomatoes or basil; shadier sills would suit salad leaves, pea shoots or herbs such as chives or chervil. A windowsill with plenty of indirect light, but no direct sun, would be a good spot for germinating seeds and raising seedlings. But windowsills are likely to be too small for large plants such as squashes or currants.

Note that plants on a windowsill receive light from one direction only. They may grow wonky and weak as they stretch towards the light, so give your pots and containers a quarter turn every few days.

Some windowsills can also be cool and draughty: the glass itself can get chilly; temperatures drop at night; and opening windows will cause jolts in temperature. So move plants back from the glass, if possible, so that they continue to receive light but enjoy a more stable and benign environment.

Lack of wind is another important consideration. Outdoors, the movement of air toughens up plants so they grow more stocky and resilient; indoor plants are less tough. (If you looked under a microscope, outdoor plants have more numerous and smaller cells, which improves texture, taste and shelf life.) The solution is to stroke your plants. Mimic the action of the wind by brushing them every time you walk by.

Outdoor windowsills

Considerations are similar to those of indoor windowsills (see above), with the key exception of the lower temperatures. Outdoor windowsills may therefore be unsuitable for germinating seeds and for tender plants that require extra warmth and protection. But they have the advantage of letting you grow trailing plants such as nasturtiums.

Take care that pots, window boxes and containers are securely attached, particularly if you are high up or in a windy site. One method is to fasten a length of wire to vine eyes in the side walls to hold them in, or to box in the whole ledge with timber.

If growing in window boxes, consider the aesthetics and weight when the container is full of compost. I sometimes use empty window boxes more as a trough for holding pots. With this method, you can slot pots into the window box, saving on weight, and allowing you to switch and rearrange plants as you fancy.

To increase your growing space, look into various devices such as adjustable brackets that allow you to fit extra window boxes over the lip of the window ledge. You could also attach pot holders to the walls, or use vine eyes or brackets for hanging baskets.

Rooftops

Blessed with direct sunlight, these dream plots are the great untapped resource for urban agriculture. But you absolutely need four things, however tempting your space may appear: structural strength, good access, water and protection from the elements. Without these, it's doomed.

If you are contemplating a new space and have any doubts about its ability to bear weight, seek expert advice. (Structural engineers or surveyors can issue a report.) It's also wise to position heavy containers on load-bearing walls and beams. Note that plants growing in containers can be very heavy, especially when watered, so choose a lightweight container material and compost mix (see charts, pages 172 and 175).

If water is an issue, install a tap – the novelty of lugging watering cans soon fades. Alternatively, run a hose to the roof that you can attach to a tap indoors.

Also, be wary of the wind: it dries out plants quickly and cold winds can upset plants, especially fruiting crops. More extreme weather can even wreck your

Ingenious use of space on a windowsill in Paris

garden. Think about using windbreaks of trellising, willow screening, netting or other similar materials, attaching them to walls, parapets or other stable structures. You can also use living windbreaks of tough hardy plants. Position your more vulnerable plants in sheltered spots.

If the roof is a sun trap, you may want to add some shelter – for both you and your plants. You can buy sail-shaped fabric screens for this purpose, or make your own.

Balconies

Balconies come in all shapes and sizes – from high-rise, south-facing suntraps to low-level, gloomy ledges. Depending on your space, balconies often share the same characteristics as windowsills and roof gardens and suit similar crops. Supports and railings can also provide handy support for climbing plants.

If wind is an issue, create windbreaks (see advice for roof gardens) and try growing more compact or dwarf varieties of plants, which are less likely get blown around. To maximise your space, add shelves or brackets to grow plants at different levels (see advice for outdoor windowsills).

Patios

Often paved, these ground-level plots are ideal for growing in pots and containers. If you have the space, consider building raised beds – frames of timber, brick or similar materials which are filled with soil or compost. You can then tailor the mix to suit the plants you want to grow. Raised beds also allow for easy access and efficient growing, as you can move around them without treading on the soil or bending too low, and pack them full with plants.

Alternatively, prise up loose paving slabs if you want grow plants direct in the ground, although you may

Les Jardins du Ruisseau,
a community garden in Paris

need to replace any poor quality soil below. I've seen this work well for herbs such as thyme or mint and even a gnarly grape vine.

Exploit the vertical dimension of the patio space, using your sunniest walls or fences for climbers such as peas, mouse melons or squashes. You may need to erect trellis or similar to provide them with support. (Always leave at least 15cm between the trellis and the wall to provide a habitat for wildlife.)

To increase light levels, consider removing any branches or even whole trees that shield the sun. Painting walls in pale colours will also reflect light.

Community gardens

These wonderful shared spaces are growing in number. Groups of like-minded souls work together to reclaim scraps of disused land in their neighbourhood. For many people without a plot of their own, community gardens provide a priceless alternative.

Investigate if there are any in your local area. Models of use vary between gardens: some are open to the public, others distribute keys to members; plots may be shared or individual.

Whatever their shape and size, community gardens are an inspiring resource and an effective way to bring local people together. After all, gardening is the least threatening and most cooperative of activities. People can swap seeds, plants and advice. There are often regular work days, harvest celebrations and a programme of events.

Allotments

Allotments are now in high demand in many urban areas. If you have one already, count yourself lucky. If you want an allotment, investigate local options that are close to home but don't be tempted to commit to a plot that involves more than a fifteen minute journey – long trips will make it a struggle. Maintaining a full-size allotment requires significant work. It can be sensible to share an allotment, or begin with a smaller 'starter' plot.

GARDENING ESSENTIALS

TOP TIPS

1   The daily patrol

A swift daily check on your plot makes all the difference, tuning you in to your plants. I do mine each morning with a first cup of strong tea. Check if anything needs watering or harvesting, or for signs of pests and disease such as nibbled leaves. Tug up weeds and graze as you go. In Japan, the nutritional advice from the government is to eat thirty different foods every day. This makes perfect sense to me, and the daily patrol is a great way to start.

2   Use your mobile

Set up reminders or alarms on your phone: to feed your chillies every fortnight, perhaps, or sow another batch of coriander. Keep a to-do list of garden tasks. If you are feeling keen, it may also prove useful to note seed germination times or how much a plant yields.

3   Read the leaves

Leaves are a mirror to plant health. Drooping or curled leaves, for example, may indicate that a plant is thirsty. A purplish tinge around the leaf edge signals a nutrient deficiency, often of nitrogen, so the plant requires feeding. Slime trails are clues to a slug or snail attack. Observe carefully and work out what your plants need.

4   Colour and shape

Green can dominate in an edible garden, especially in shady urban plots where some flowers may struggle to flourish. Blocks or lines of one crop may also prove visually dull. Mix up the colours – for example, by growing nasturtiums or crimson beetroots amongst your veg. Vary shape and structure by sowing and planting in drifts, curves and circles.

5   Test and trial

Which compost do tomatoes like best? What pea variety offers the highest yield? Gardening throws up endless questions, so get in the habit of running informal tests and trials. Jot down any details and results – I'm often convinced I won't forget, only to scratch my head in confusion a few weeks later.

Sowing seeds

Seeds are living things, itching to grow. They are waiting for us to provide the triggers to break their dormancy — heat, moisture, air and (in most cases) darkness.

The temperature at which seed will germinate varies between plants. Peas, for example, respond to a much lower range of temperatures than chillies. As a guide, it always helps to imagine in what climate the plant grows best.

There are various techniques for sowing seeds. I often start mine off in plug trays, then later plant out the seedlings into containers or the ground. You can also sow seeds directly where they will grow. The simplest method for direct sowing is to scatter them evenly over an area. This is called 'broadcasting'. You can also sow in straight lines or drills. Another option is to station sow, which means planting seeds at a set distance apart from each other. This reduces the need to thin out later, removing some of the seedlings so that the remainder has sufficient space in which to grow on.

With all methods, make sure that you have prepared the soil or compost before sowing. Break up any lumps, aiming for a fine tilth of loose soil to make life easier for the germinating seed and young plant. Remove any stones or debris and tug up any weeds.

As a rule of thumb, the depth that you sow seeds into soil or compost is twice their diameter. Take care not to sow too thickly, as this overcrowds plants and creates extra work. Let seed packets be your guide to the specific requirements of each plant.

Raising seedlings

I suggest using plug trays, also known as cells or modules. This method – using a sort of compartmentalised seed tray – gives your plants the best possible start. Crucially, it makes efficient use of space too: you can start off a large number of plants in a small area, where it's easy to monitor their progress, and then plant them out at exactly the right spacing. This also avoids thinning out and allows you to fill gaps as soon as a previous crop is over, saving precious weeks of growing time.

Of course, there are endless other methods for raising seedlings – using either shop-bought items or recycled and improvised materials. Pots or similar containers, for example, do the trick perfectly well. Experiment and discover what works best for you.

Hardening off

This is a key technique if you start growing your plants indoors before moving them outdoors to grow on. Hardening off is a process of gradual acclimatization for the harsher life outside. It encourages the plant cells to become tougher and more numerous, and the leaves to develop a thicker protective coat. If you don't harden off plants, the colder and fluctuating temperatures, combined with the force of the chilling wind, can shock vulnerable plants – stalling growth or even killing them outright.

The process is simple: you just incrementally increase your plants' exposure to outside conditions. The exact duration depends on how much difference there is between indoor and outdoor temperatures, but a fortnight is a good rule of thumb.

I start by moving plug trays of plants outdoors during the day, then back inside at night, gradually cranking up the duration. During the second week I leave them out at night, at first covered with a blanket of newspaper or a double layer of horticultural fleece (a fabric for protecting plants) if it's cold. If you have a greenhouse or cold frame, these make an ideal staging post.

Hardening off is particularly essential for tender plants such as chillies or courgettes, which should go outside only when there is no more chance of frost. But don't fret if you can't always manage it systematically; just do your best. Let's face it – life sometimes gets in the way.

Watering

It's a simple task, but often rushed or forgotten. Plants do suffer if you regularly subject them to water stress – leaves droop as they take emergency measures by closing pores in their leaves to reduce water loss. The plants then take some time to recover, which stalls growth.

A good soak is far better than a quick sprinkle. If we water too swiftly we moisten only the top layer of the soil or compost. Roots are therefore encouraged to grow shallow, rather than stretching deep. This makes for a weaker and less resilient plant. We will also need to water more frequently.

Seedlings, of course, require delicate watering. Use a fine rose, the spray attachment on hoses and watering cans. You can also make or buy special devices for fine watering which you attach to recycled water bottles. Plants in pots and containers will also need extra attention (see page 173).

Weeding

Keep on top of weeds – show them who is boss. Pull them up as you garden, ideally with roots intact. This chore is much easier when weeds are young, before they get a chance to establish themselves. Never allow weeds to flower and set seed, as this will create much more work in seasons to come. As the old saying goes, 'One year's seeding means seven years' weeding.'

Fertilising and feeding

This can be a confusing area. In shops and garden centres you can buy dozens of products to feed plants: some are chemically synthesised; others are marketed as organic. (See the section on organic growing, page 167). There is also a wide gamut of organic plant foods you can make yourself, such as garden compost or comfrey juice, which is made by diluting the juice extracted from fermented leaves of the comfrey plant.

In this book, I will keep it simple: fertilisers are solids, often pellets or powders, and release their nutrients more slowly than feeds, which are liquids. It's best to use liquid feeds for plants in pots and containers. Fertilisers are best for plants growing in the soil.

Whatever the product or preparation, essentially two types are most useful. General-purpose fertilisers and feeds, either chemical or organic, suit leafy crops and provide a wide spectrum of nutrients. Some are also used to boost the nutrients in soil or compost before growing plants.

For fruiting plants – for example, tomatoes or chillies after flowering – it's best to switch to a food that has extra potassium as this helps with the fruit development. These products are sometimes called high-potassium or high-potash – tomato foods are the most common example and can be used on other plants too.

Dissolved nutrients in water enter plant cells through the process of osmosis and an excess of nutrients will actually harm the plant, causing imbalances and blocking the plant from accessing other nutrients. Too much nitrogen, for example, promotes the growth of weak foliage prone to pest attack. Always read the label of shop-bought feeds and fertilisers and use at the correct dosage and frequency.

Pinching out the side shoots from a tomato plant

Pinching out

A simple technique with a huge impact. Pinching out or stopping is a way to grow bushier, more compact plants, which saves space and boosts your harvest. It is very simple – use your fingernails to pinch out the growing tip, the tallest and most vigorous main shoot of the plant. Remove it just above a leaf node, the place where the leaves attach to the stem.

The plant will then redirect its energy into growing larger and more numerous side shoots, bulking up the plant. You can repeat this process several times as the plant grows, and try it on large side shoots too. Pinching out works well with basil, lemon verbena, shiso, shungiku and chillies and is recommended for some types of tomato (see page 56).

A fine crop of mixed radishes
from a school garden

VEGETABLES

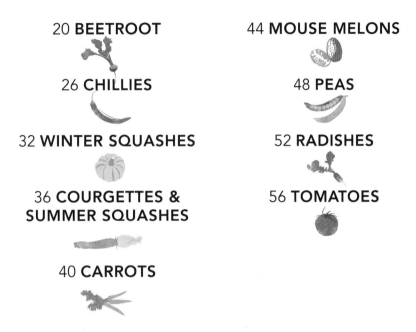

20 **BEETROOT**

26 **CHILLIES**

32 **WINTER SQUASHES**

36 **COURGETTES & SUMMER SQUASHES**

40 **CARROTS**

44 **MOUSE MELONS**

48 **PEAS**

52 **RADISHES**

56 **TOMATOES**

This selection includes some of my favourite plants – all are winners on the urban plot. 'Vegetable' is a word we commonly use to describe plants that we like to eat. Botanists, however, would shudder at this lazy use of language because this term does not pinpoint which plant part we consume: with carrots, for example, it's the roots; with peas, we mostly eat the seeds and pods – the fruit of the plant.

As you garden, explore which bits of your edible plants are best to eat – you may be surprised. With radishes, for example, the roots, leaves, flowers and seed pods are all edible, although the stem is too fibrous and chewy.

When we grow our own, we can control the size at which we will harvest our crops – for me, this is one of the greatest perks. Baby courgettes and beetroots, for example, are far superior to the monsters we are asked to buy. We can also pick at the perfect moment of ripeness – tomatoes are superb straight off the vine.

In this section, you will find my best plants for small areas. Asparagus, garlic, kale, kohl rabi and turnips are also well worth a try. Beans would be another good choice if you want a plant that climbs into vertical spaces. New potatoes are delightful, but these large plants require plenty of room.

Beta vulgaris

BEETROOT

Nothing beats a beetroot for colour. That lush deep purple looks ravishing on a plate; other varieties are shades of gold or striped with white.

Beetroots are easy and fast to grow, and are best picked when small. The leaves are also delicious, although often discarded. A Bangladeshi lady once spotted me harvesting just the roots. She gave me a pitying look, pointed out my mistake, and took the leaves home for her supper.

In the kitchen, beetroot has a remarkable earthy sweetness, quite unlike the crude, vinegar-soaked roots you may remember, with a shudder, from childhood.

Recommended varieties Grow a mix of colours: 'Chioggia' or 'Candy Stripe' is pink-and-white-striped (note that the stripes wash out when cooked); 'Burpees Golden' is a delicious heritage variety with orange skin and yellow flesh, so won't stain your fingers or cooking water; 'Detroit White' is lighter in colour; 'Boltardy' is an excellent round purple beetroot, with some resistance to bolting; 'Cheltenham Green Top' is more tapered in shape, with excellent flavour. The bold crimson of 'Bull's Blood' makes it the perfect variety for salad leaves and also brings colour to your plot.

Growing The seed itself is large, with a thick coat, so an overnight soak in warm water before sowing will hasten germination, but is not essential. Sow from mid-spring to late summer in a sunny spot, directly where the plant is to grow, and thin out later if necessary. Alternatively, sow into plug trays, one seed per cell, then plant out as seedlings. Sow a new batch every month for a steady supply. Note that beetroot grows happily in a clump, so you can also sow three or four seeds together to make efficient use of space. Late-summer sowings will provide a winter supply. *Spacing:* From 8cm for small beetroot to 20cm for large specimens. Allow about 30cm between rows. If growing solely for leaves, you can squeeze plants more closely together.

Containers *Minimum compost depth:* 20cm. Beetroot does fine in multipurpose compost. Either sow direct into containers or plant seedlings. You can use the foliage of beetroot to add colour in a container display of mixed plants. *Indoors:* Possible for small roots, space permitting, but better suited to baby salad leaves – sow seed thickly and harvest when small and tender.

roots, leaves

3/5

In the ground Beetroot prefers a light and reasonably fertile soil but is not too fussy.

Harvesting Pull roots when young, small and tender. Old roots turn woody. With clumps, twist out the larger beetroots, leaving the remainder to grow on.

Seed saving Not straightforward: beetroots produce seed in the second year of their life cycle, and will cross with other related plants nearby.

Pests and diseases Slugs may target seedlings, but beetroot is otherwise largely trouble-free.

Preserving Pickle any surplus. For example, boil until cooked but still firm, then peel, slice and cover with a pickling vinegar spiced with orange zest, cloves, coriander seeds and cinnamon. Alternatively, pickle raw, in small cubes or shaved into slivers (see page 182). Polish-style grated beetroot and horseradish relish is another winning combination.

Notes

Beetroot is in the Chenopodiaceae family, also known as goosefoots, and is closely related to chard. It is a biennial, with a two-year life cycle, although we eat the roots in their first year.

Beetroot leaves are both colourful and ornamental, so can be striking when used to edge beds or divide up a plot.

Hot weather can trigger the plants into starting the flowering stage of their life cycle. This undesirable process is called bolting and diverts the plant's energy. Keep well watered in hot weather, which helps to lower the soil temperature. Certain varieties also offer some resistance to bolting.

7 WAYS WITH BEETROOT

Show off beetroot's fine colours. Play around with texture, too, by grating beetroot raw, shaving it into slivers, or even sautéing in small cubes. Whole beetroot can be roasted, boiled or steamed. Cooking times range between half an hour for baby roots to two hours for whoppers. I prefer roasting, which concentrates flavour and sweetness. Note that eating beetroot can turn your urine red – it's harmless, so don't worry!

For salads, add leaves when young and tender. Marinate the roots in the dressing before mixing with other ingredients so that they soak up the flavours. It's also wise to add cut purple beetroot to any dish at the last minute, to avoid staining. Beetroot pairs especially well with dill, mint, anchovy, coconut, cumin, capers, horseradish, goat's cheese and orange.

❀ To roast beetroot, twist off the leaves, wash the roots and then wrap each root loosely in kitchen foil. For extra flavour, add thyme, a pinch of sea salt, crushed garlic and a splash of balsamic or red wine vinegar. Cook in an oven at 200°c/400°F/gas 6 for 30–40 minutes, or until you can pierce them with a fork. (Exact timing depends on the size.) With very large beetroots, speed up the process by chopping in half and wrapping each individually. On a barbecue, you can use this same foil method but parboil the beetroot first.

❀ To boil beetroot, twist off the leaves but keep the root itself intact to prevent the colour from leaching. Boil the roots whole, until you can pierce them with a fork.

❀ For a sumptuous, slow-cooked dish, bake a beetroot gratin, either mixing slices with potato, as in recipes for a classic Dauphinois, or going alone with the beetroot.

❀ For salads, try mixing cooked beetroot with mustard leaves, cracked hazelnuts or walnuts, crumbled feta cheese, mint and a sprinkle of lemon juice. Alternatively, peel and grate raw beetroot and carrots, then mix with dill or coriander, cumin and orange juice, and garnish with chives.

❀ Add cooked beetroot and a touch of horseradish when mashing potato.

❀ Add young leaves raw to salads.

❀ To cook the leaves, sauté in butter or olive oil with a little garlic, fresh ginger and a splash of apple juice. Cover and cook for 2 minutes, or until softened. My favourite method is with raisins and pine nuts, Majorcan style: soak raisins in warm water or sherry; roast pine nuts and allow to cool; sauté onion and garlic until soft, then add chopped beetroot leaves, a squeeze of orange juice and the soaked raisins, cover and cook as above. Stir through the pine nuts, season and serve.

BEETROOT & TAHINI

This delicious recipe from Lebanon is a favourite from my friend Anissa Helou's book Modern Mezze. *I rate tahini, a paste of ground sesame seeds, as an essential standby ingredient — it's versatile, widely available and stores for ages in the fridge. Serve the beetroot as a starter or with a mixture of dishes for a mezze lunch.*

Roast the beetroot first (see opposite). To make the dressing, measure the tahini into a bowl and stir in half the lemon juice and 100ml of cold water until well combined. Then gradually stir in more of lemon juice, tasting as you go, aiming for the consistency of double cream. Add the garlic and salt, again to taste.

Chop the cooked beetroot into slices about 5mm thick and arrange on a plate. Add a swoosh of the tahini dressing and sprinkle with the herbs.

Serves 4–6, as a side dish

800g beetroot (approx.), roasted and
  peeled
2 tablespoons chopped mint, dill
  or parsley, to garnish
For the tahini dressing:
150ml tahini
Juice of 1½ lemons (or to taste)
1 garlic clove, crushed to a paste
Sea salt

Clockwise from top:
Slivers of 'Burpees Golden', 'Boltardy',
'Chioggia' and 'Albina Vereduna'

BEETROOT LEAF CURRY

Serves 2, as a small main course

2 tablespoons vegetable oil
1 medium-sized onion, finely chopped
2 garlic cloves, finely chopped
½ teaspoon salt
150g raw shelled prawns
½ teaspoon turmeric
½ teaspoon paprika
½ teaspoon masala
6 tablespoons water
200g beetroot leaves (approx.), chopped

This is a spicy finale for beetroot leaves — an authentic Bangladeshi prawn curry. It comes courtesy of my friend Rubina, whose mother is a nifty cook. The spices include masala, a blend of powdered mixed spices. Garam masala is a popular example. Masalas are widely available under various brand names — just use whichever mix you can find. Serve the curry with rice, on its own, or with a spread of other curries. You can also add sorrel, mustard or spinach leaves if you fancy.

In a heavy-based pan, heat the oil, then fry the onion, garlic and salt over a medium heat until they start to colour. Add the prawns and cook for 3–6 minutes, stirring occasionally, until the prawns are cooked — timing will depend on their size. Add the turmeric, paprika and masala, stir well and fry for a further minute. Pour in the water, stir again, then add the beetroot leaves and cook, covered, for 3–4 minutes, or until the leaves are soft. Stir in an extra tablespoon or two of water if you want more sauce. Stir well before serving. Eat immediately.

Capsicum annuum, C. baccatum, C, chinense, C. frutescens, C. pubescens

CHILLIES

Watch out – growing chillies is addictive. I've seen otherwise sensible gardeners become obsessed, move to the countryside and buy a polytunnel to farm myriad varieties.

If you have a sunny spot, definitely grow them. Chillies are both edible and decorative, do very well indoors, and one plant will enhance a few dozen dinners.

The tricky bit is choosing varieties. Chillies come in many shapes, sizes, colours, degrees of heat and distinct flavours. In fact, the milder types are better thought of as a vegetable rather than a spice. Some countries, such as Mexico, understand their subtleties, but the rest of us still have a lot to learn.

Recommended varieties The choice of varieties can be bewildering so focus on choosing a suitable plant to match your climate and plot. Look online for specialist chilli nurseries and ask them for recommendations. If growing outside, make sure the chillies are listed as 'outdoor' varieties suitable for your area. 'Super Chilli' is well worth trying. For indoor windowsills and similar spots, choose compact or dwarf varieties such as 'Apache F1'. 'Hungarian Hot Wax' is medium hot, easy to grow and an early cropper. 'Habanero' chillies are hotter, with excellent flavour. Look out for Peruvian 'Aji' chillies, such as 'Aji Crystal', which have a stunning lemony edge. For wonderful colour, consider purple-fruited varieties such as 'Purple Venezuelan'.

Growing Chillies require a warm, sunny spot and a long growing season to bear fruit. So decide if you will grow from seed, starting very early in the season – at least a month ahead of most other crops. Alternatively, take the short cut of buying established plants later in spring, which will spare you the steps below.

Sow seed into small pots or plug trays, one seed per cell, in late winter or very early spring. They need warmth to germinate. Optimum temperature varies (check the seed packet or supplier), but lies in the range of 21–27°c. Choose a snug spot, such as above a radiator, an airing cupboard or in a heated propagator. Germination can take up to three weeks.

Temperature becomes slightly less vital once the seed has germinated. Nevertheless, continue to raise the seedlings in a warm, bright spot

fruit 5/5

indoors, potting up the plants at least twice whenever the roots outgrow their current container. You can check if it's time to do this by sliding the plant out of its pot to see if the roots have taken up all available space. Then transfer the plant into a pot with a slightly larger diameter, adding fresh compost. *Spacing:* About 50cm between plants

Containers *Minimum compost depth:* 20cm. As they grow, chillies should be potted up. The final container should be at least 25–30cm in diameter. Chillies are happy in a standard multipurpose compost. Use a general-purpose liquid feed, switching to a high-potassium feed when the plants start to produce fruit. *Indoors:* Chillies make splendid houseplants: reserve your sunniest windowsill. When they start to flower, assist pollination by gently shaking the plants or rubbing a cotton bud around inside each flower. This mimics the action of wind and insects.

In the ground Harden off the plants (see page 16) before moving them permanently outside in late spring when they start to flower.

Harvesting
Most chillies mature from green to red, but intermediate shades are common. They taste more grassy and herbaceous when green, fruitier and hotter when red – pick at the stage you desire. Keep harvesting to encourage the plant to produce more fruit. Pick from lower branches first.

Seed saving
Not straightforward. Chillies will cross-pollinate, so grow only one variety if you want to try saving seed. Let the chillies ripen fully on the plant. Pick and cut off the flesh, then further dry the seedy core before picking out the seed using gloves and tweezers. Sow the following season, as viability declines swiftly.

Pests and diseases
Chillies are generally trouble-free outdoors. Aphids may target young leaves. On plants grown indoors, red spider mite and whitefly are possible pests (see page 165).

Preserving
To freeze, dice into handy portions and freeze in ice-cube trays, without water. You can also dry chillies in a low oven, which will take 10–20 minutes, depending on size. Alternatively, thread dried chillies for a garland, make a chilli jam, pickle them whole, or freeze in a chilli butter with coriander and lime (see page 182).

Notes
Chillies are often grown as annuals but can be perennials in native countries. They are in the Solanaceae family, which includes tomatoes and peppers.

You want a bushy, compact plant with balanced branches, so if the plant is looking at all spindly pinch out the growing tip and side shoots when the bush is about 20–30cm high (see page 17).

Chillies do not enjoy wet 'feet', so be careful not to overwater.

You can try to overwinter favourite plants to get a head start the next growing season. In late autumn, move the plant to a warm, bright spot indoors. Cut the main stem down to 10–15cm and reduce watering to a minimum. The plant may go dormant and look more dead than alive. In spring, repot in fresh compost and snip off dead growth.

5 WAYS WITH CHILLIES

The heat of a chilli varies hugely depending on the variety. To check, slice open, touch the inner flesh and tentatively taste. The hottest part of the chilli is the membrane attaching the seeds to the flesh – scrape out with a knife if necessary. Don't bother deseeding milder chillies. Take care when handling chopped chillies – use gloves or wash your fingers thoroughly. Try mixing and matching varieties for the perfect blend of flavours. Chillies pair especially well with chocolate, coconut, squashes, coriander and mint.

✿ For a snack with milder chillies, slice in half lengthways and stuff with a mixture of a melty cheese, breadcrumbs and herbs, then flash under the grill until golden and crisp.

✿ For a starter or quick lunch, treat yourself to a buffalo mozzarella or burrata cheese. Tear the cheese into chunks, then sprinkle it with finely diced red chilli (to taste), cracked pepper, your best olive oil and perhaps some herbs for colour. You could also serve this on bruschetta or crostini.

✿ To make the best hot chocolate, chop good-quality dark chocolate into chunks and set aside. In a saucepan, warm a cup of milk per person, turn off the heat, then add a mild chilli, sliced lengthways, and cinnamon to taste, and allow to infuse for at least 10 minutes. Strain half the milk into another pan, gently heat and whisk in the chopped chocolate until melted. Top up with the remaining milk until it's the consistency you like. A splash or rum or Cointreau is a decadent addition.

✿ To jazz up a tropical fruit salad, marinate the fruit in a spicy sugar syrup infused with chilli, star anise, cloves, pink peppercorns and fresh ginger (see page 128). Pour this over chopped fruit, adding mint.

✿ To make a dipping sauce, slice a chilli into rings, mix with finely diced shallot, sprinkle with salt, and splash over rice wine vinegar. Allow to marinate for at least 10 minutes. Try with spring rolls or Vietnamese summer rolls (see page 88).

CHILLI CORN BREAD

This is gorgeous warm from the oven, perhaps with a cup of coffee at breakfast or to refuel after a blast of gardening. Try it spread with butter and honey. The chillies lend a gentle heat, but because they vary in pungency test first and adjust quantities accordingly. The corn bread will keep for several days.

Preheat the oven to 200°c/400°f/gas 6. Grease a small loaf tin or 20–23cm square cake tin with olive oil. (A lining of baking parchment will also help, but is not essential.)

Deseed and finely chop the chillies, adjusting the quantity to taste. Heat a heavy-based frying pan, with no oil, then dry-roast the chillies and sweetcorn until they just begin to char and blacken.

Sift the flour and baking powder into a mixing bowl. Add the chillies, sweetcorn and remaining dry ingredients, then mix thoroughly together. Separate any lumps of sugar with your fingers.

In a separate bowl, briefly whisk together the wet ingredients. Tip this mixture into the dry ingredients and whisk again until combined. Pour into the greased tin and bake for 25–35 minutes, depending on tin size, or until cooked through and golden. Test by inserting a skewer into the centre of the bread, which should emerge clean if the bread is cooked. Allow to cool, then tip out and serve.

Serves 4

Olive oil, for greasing

For the dry ingredients:
2 mild red chillies (or to taste)
80g sweetcorn, tinned or thawed from frozen
100g plain flour
2 teaspoons baking powder
200g coarse polenta or corn meal
30g light brown sugar
½ teaspoon ground cumin
½ teaspoon freshly ground pepper
½ teaspoon salt

For the wet ingredients:
300ml soured cream or yoghurt
100ml olive oil
2 eggs, lightly beaten

SALSA MEXICANA

This simple, fresh salsa takes seconds to make. I first tried it in a street café in Mexico, where an ancient lady sold me a small bag of dynamite ground 'Habanero' chilli – the tiniest sprinkle blasts your socks off.

Use a really sharp knife to dice the ingredients finely. Play around by adding a few drops of cider vinegar or red wine vinegar, a pinch of ground cumin, or slivers of radish and spring onion. Eat fresh and serve with tortilla chips or grilled meat.

Mix all the ingredients except the coriander. Let the flavours mingle for an hour. Add the coriander just before serving.

Serves 2

1 fresh mild chilli (or to taste), deseeded and very finely diced
½ small onion, finely diced
1 ripe medium-sized tomato, deseeded and finely diced
Juice of 2 limes
Pinch of caster sugar
Pinch of salt
Few drops of sesame oil
2 tablespoons chopped coriander leaves

Cucurbita maxima, C. mixta, C. moschata, C. pepo

WINTER SQUASHES

Stuffed with character, winter squashes make me hesitate – some are simply too beautiful to go straight for the chop. I love their heavy, cool weight in my hands. They often decorate my kitchen through the winter, then I scoff them just before they go soft.

Winter squashes are related to summer squashes, but have a harder skin and can be stored for months. The plants are swift to grow and touchingly keen to scramble and climb into unloved places. They do need room – a few metres or so – to stretch outwards or upwards, or coil into a spiralling circle.

I've grown squashes along hedges, around doorways and arches and on a neglected patch on a local estate in a spot of guerrilla gardening. Bangladeshi friends often grow the prized pale green 'Dudhi' squash over trellised frames on their balconies, gardens and patios.

There are hundreds of varieties, in all shapes and colours, so a squash addiction will last a lifetime.

Recommended varieties From the many varieties take care to choose one that matches your growing space. Among the smaller squashes, try the dinky 'Munchkin', which is just the right size for a single serving. The medium-sized 'Sweet Dumpling' has pretty stripes and a fine texture. The larger 'Hokkaido', also known as 'Kuri', is available in various colours and has a nutty flavour. The pale blue 'Crown Prince' has delicious sweet flesh. For a more decorative squash for Halloween, try 'Jack-O-Lantern' or the smaller 'Baby Bear'.

Growing First, reserve your growing area. Squashes relish a sunny spot with plenty of space. Remember you can train smaller varieties of squash upwards, tying in and letting them cling to trellis, netting, wigwams or similar structures.

Sow two seeds per small pot in late spring. Choose somewhere warm for germination, around 20°c. Remove the weaker plant at seedling stage. *Spacing:* 1–2m, depending on variety.

Containers *Minimum compost depth:* 30cm. Not ideal, because of size. If you must, use your largest container and choose smaller varieties. Keep well watered and support the fruit if necessary. *Indoors:* Not suitable.

In the ground Prepare your planting hole in advance. Dig in garden

fruit, flowers, seeds, leaves

1/5

compost, vermicompost, well-rotted manure, leaf mould or other organic matter to retain moisture. Once the soil has warmed up, harden off the squashes (see page 16), then plant in their final position.

Harvesting Harvest as late as possible but before the first frost. (Frosted squashes may look fine, but the flesh is damaged.) A hard skin, even colouring and cracks in the stem are all indicators that the fruit is ripe. Use a sharp knife to cut the fruit away, including a few centimetres of stalk. Leave to harden further for up to two weeks in a dry, light spot outside. Then store indoors somewhere cool and dry, with decent air circulation.

Seed saving Not straightforward or recommended. Varieties of squash will cross-pollinate, so you need to pollinate by hand.

Pests and diseases Slugs and snails may target seedlings. Powdery mildew can be a problem in dry conditions: symptoms include white, dusty patches on the leaves (see page 165).

Preserving Squashes can store from two to six months or more depending on the variety. Watch out for blemishes or squishy patches. If you have a glut, use for chutney or purée and freeze. To transform them into an ornament, carve and varnish the fruits with shellac, a traditional varnish.

Notes

Winter squashes are half-hardy annuals in the Cucurbitaceae family, which includes courgettes, cucumbers and mouse melons. Plants produce both male and female flowers, although only the females bear fruit (see page 37 for how to distinguish between the two).

Squashes rely on insects for pollination. If in doubt, pollinate by hand, transferring pollen from the male to female flowers. You can use a cotton bud or small paintbrish, or simply pick a male flower, pick off the leaves and dab the pollen from the anther onto the stigma of the female flower.

Unlike summer squashes (see page 36), winter squashes are harvested when fully mature and store for months.

Squashes are useful for smothering weeds as they have large leaves and grow very quickly.

When watering, soak around the base of the plant but try not to wet the plant itself. One tactic is to sink an upended plastic water bottle, with the bottom cut off, into the soil beside the plant. Water poured into the bottle will be channelled to the roots.

'Stop' the plants after they form about three fruits by removing new emerging flowers. This diverts the plant's energy into ripening the remaining fruit. Cut away leaves that are shading the fruit, and ideally shuffle a tile or brick under the fruit to absorb heat, reduce the risk of water damage and hasten the ripening process.

5 WAYS WITH WINTER SQUASHES

Peeling squashes is fiddly and often unnecessary, for example when roasting. Use a vegetable peeler if you must: slice off the bottom first, to provide a stable base. Then cut in half lengthways and scoop out the seeds with a spoon. As with courgettes, the flowers and young leaves are edible. The seeds can be also roasted.

Be extra generous with herbs and spices, as squash flesh can soak up flavour. Squashes combine especially well with rosemary, sage, thyme, chilli, ginger, garlic, cinnamon, cloves, nutmeg, and crushed coriander, fennel or cumin seeds.

❁ To roast, chop squash into crescents and rub the flesh with oil or butter and spices, as above. My favourite mix is chilli flakes and ground cinnamon. Cook at 220°c/425°f/gas 7 for 30–40 minutes, or until soft and golden. Alternatively, roast with sage, serving with shavings of Parmesan or pecorino cheese. The seeds will roast alongside if left with the squash.

❁ Steam chunks of peeled squash. Season and eat unadorned, or mash with extras such as feta cheese, grated fresh ginger, spring onions and butter.

❁ Make a squash purée for babies or for chef-like flourishes for posh suppers. Roast or steam, allow to cool, scoop out the flesh, blitz and season, adding butter, cream or tahini if you wish.

❁ Roast the seeds for a tasty snack. Rinse, then spread on an oiled baking tray in an oven at about 140°c /275°f/gas 1 for 10 minutes, or until dry. (I often use the lingering heat after roasting.) Transfer to a frying pan and dry-roast without oil over low heat until they start to colour. In a swift motion, add a tiny splash of water, stir, then sprinkle with a pinch of salt. The water helps the salt to stick to the seeds. Alternatively, try light soy sauce instead of the water and salt. Other spices are optional.

❁ Squashes make stunning serving bowls: a large specimen can be a centrepiece; smaller squashes suit individual servings. Cook the filling separately and bake the hollowed-out squash until cooked. Stuff the squash with fillings such as couscous and rice mixes, and warm through in the oven.

SQUASH & COCONUT SOUP

This is a tropical and warming soup, spiked with coconut, curry powder, ginger and cinnamon. Try grating paper-thin ribbons of raw squash over each bowl before serving to add a juicy crunch. A sprinkle of greenery — coriander leaves or grated lime zest, perhaps — will add colour.

Preheat the oven to 190°c/375°F/gas 5. Halve the squash lengthways, peel, discard the seeds, chop into crescents (save one for grating later), then chop into even-sized chunks. Place the chunks in a roasting tray and toss with the olive oil and thyme leaves. Roast for 20–30 minutes, or until soft and starting to turn brown and caramelise.

Transfer to a saucepan, add half of the stock and blitz with a stick blender. (Alternatively, transfer to a blender, blitz and then return to the pan.) Adjust the consistency by adding more stock and extra water, if needed.

Cook over a low heat, tasting as you go, finely grate in the ginger and creamed coconut and gradually add the curry powder — make sure you do not overdo the spicing. Stir, taste again, and season with the cinnamon, salt and pepper. Simmer gently for 1 minute to let the flavours mingle. Pour into bowls, and use the widest aperture of a grater or mandolin to grate over one or two thin ribbons of raw squash from the reserved crescent. Add the coriander or lime zest to garnish and serve hot.

Serves 2

1 squash (approx. 700g–1kg)
2 tablespoons olive oil
¼ teaspoon thyme leaves
400ml vegetable stock
1 thumbnail-sized piece of fresh ginger, peeled
Creamed coconut (to taste)
½ teaspoon curry powder (or to taste)
Pinch of ground cinnamon
Pinch of salt
Pinch of pepper
Coriander leaves or strips of lime zest, to garnish

Note that the recipe calls for creamed coconut, sold in a block. A splash of thick coconut milk is a decent replacement.

Cucurbita pepo

COURGETTES & SUMMER SQUASHES

Brazen and generous, courgettes and their summer squash sisters are great fun to grow. The plants pump out their large, bright yellow flowers all summer as an irresistible siren to local insects. Harvest a few of these fragile delicacies as a special treat.

The courgette fruits themselves grow amazingly quickly – pick often, when they are small, firm and crunchy. At this stage they are far superior to anything you will find in the shops.

There is a wonderful variety to choose from: round or slim, smooth or knobbly, in shades from near black to white. 'Patty Pans', a related summer squash, look more like flying saucers. 'Tromboncino' bears bizarre wonky fruit and can be encouraged to climb upwards. All need a decent chunk of space on the plot.

Recommended varieties Note that courgettes and summer squashes have thinner skin than winter squashes, and are eaten fresh rather than stored. Match the variety to your growing space: some plants are compact, others more sprawling. 'Romanesco' is a ridged courgette, with excellent flavour and texture. 'Supremo F1' is particularly suitable for small spaces. Rounder types include 'Tondo di Nizza' and 'Eight Ball F1'. For yellow courgettes, which are easier to spot and bring colour to the plot, try 'Soleil F1' and 'Goldrush F1'. 'Tromboncino', also known as 'Tromba', suits vertical growing. 'Patty Pans' are available in white, yellow and green. You may come across varieties that have been bred to produce more male flowers, which is useful if you want a floral surplus to harvest.

Growing Courgettes and summer squashes require a sunny spot. Always grow at least two plants to ensure pollination. Don't sow seed too early: seedlings struggle in low light levels and cool temperatures, especially at night. Later sowings will catch up and do better.

Sow two seeds per small pot, removing the weakest once germinated. Start them off in a warm and bright spot indoors in mid-spring, or outdoors about a month later, when night temperatures average 13–15°C. Sow a second batch in early summer to extend the season.
Spacing: According to variety, typically 1m between plants.

Containers *Minimum compost depth:* 25cm. These are large, thirsty

fruit, flowers, leaves

2/5

plants and may well struggle in containers. Yields will be lower than if plants are growing in the ground. Minimum container diameter is 70cm and regular watering is essential. Choose compact or dwarf varieties, and plant one per container. Create a rich compost mix, adding well-rotted manure, garden compost or vermicompost if available. Use a general-purpose liquid feed, switching to a high-potassium feed once the plants start to flower and form fruit. *Indoors:* Not suitable.

In the ground Ideally, prepare your final planting hole a few weeks in advance. Choose a sunny, sheltered spot. Dig out the hole and fork the bottom to help with drainage. Mix the excavated soil with handfuls of well-rotted manure, garden compost or vermicompost if available, then replace. You could sow seed straight into warm soil, but you run the risk of pest attack. I prefer to plant out hardened-off courgettes (see page 16), ideally with at least four pairs of leaves.

Harvesting Harvest fruit young, when 10–15cm in length, using a knife to cut cleanly from the stem. Regular picking encourages the plant to produce more flowers and fruit. For flowers, note the difference between males and females – peer inside to distinguish. The male flowers have a more slender stem and bear the pollen-bearing, pointy anther. Female flowers enclose the more bulbous and ridged stigma. Only pollinated female flowers will bear fruit, which will start to swell behind the flower. Both sexes of flower are edible, but a harvest of a female flower with an immature fruit is the ultimate delicacy.

Seed saving Not straightforward or recommended. Varieties of squash will cross-pollinate, so you need to pollinate by hand. Plants for seed saving will also produce a lower yield as the fruit requires extra weeks on the plant to ripen.

Pests and diseases Slugs often target seedlings. Mould or rots on the fruit increase during wet spells, but should ease when the weather improves. Powdery mildew may strike, leaving white, dusty patches on the leaves (see page 165). This is common at the end of their growing season and is not a great cause for concern.

Preserving Courgettes and summer squashes do freeze but the texture deteriorates. Slice and griddle first if you want to try. Alternatively, pickle with white wine vinegar or use in a chutney (see page 185).

Notes

Courgettes and summer squashes are tender annuals in the Cucurbitaceae family, which includes cucumbers, mouse melons and winter squashes. Pollination is by insects, typically bees, moving between male and female flowers. Plants produce both sexes of flower, but only the females develop fruit. It's wise to grow more than one plant as extra flowers improve the odds for successful pollination.

Water well, especially when fruit is developing. Take extra care to water around the roots, not the leaves, as courgettes are particularly susceptible to powdery mildew.

6 WAYS WITH COURGETTES & SUMMER SQUASHES

Mix up the colours of varieties, and relish the crunchy texture of the fresh, small fruits. The flowers are an occasional delicacy. The tender young leaves are also edible, chopped into curries or soups.

Larger specimens, such as marrows, are more watery than smaller fruits so require different treatment: scoop out and discard the seeds if necessary, then blanch for a few minutes in boiling water. This will soften tough skins and speed up subsequent cooking.

Courgettes and summer squashes combine especially well with basil, chives, dill, fennel, mint, parsley, tarragon, chilli, garlic, ginger and salty cheeses such as feta.

❀ For a stylish raw salad, use a wide grater or mandolin to shave courgettes into thin discs. Arrange daintily on a plate, perhaps adding crumbled goat's cheese and edible flowers. Sprinkle with sea salt and drops of your best olive oil and lemon juice.

❀ Grill strips of courgette or summer squash on the barbecue or griddle. Brush with oil first, then season with salt, pepper, lemon juice, herbs and perhaps a touch of red chilli.

❀ Deep-fry the flowers in a crisp tempura batter (see page 119). Peek inside each flower first and shake out any insects. Stuff the flowers before frying if you fancy: try ricotta cheese, lemon zest and mint, or mozzarella and anchovies. You could also fry matchsticks of the courgette fruit itself – cut firm slivers including the outer skin.

❀ Sprinkle the flowers over pizza and fold them into risottos, omelettes and quesadillas.

❀ To use up large courgettes and squashes, try fritters. Grate the firm outer flesh into a colander, sprinkle with salt, place a dish underneath, and allow the flesh to drain for half an hour. Vigorously squeeze out excess water with your hands, then mix the flesh with grated halloumi cheese. Press into small balls in the palm of your hand and deep-fry until golden. Drain on kitchen paper and serve with a favourite dip.

❀ Stew large chunks with tomatoes and spicy harissa paste. Sauté onions and garlic until soft, stir in harissa (to taste), add chunks of raw courgette or squash and a tin of tomatoes, then cook, covered, until tender. Serve in bowls with a swirl of olive oil and squeeze of lemon juice, plus plenty of crusty white bread to mop up the juices.

SUMMER SALAD

This superb salad stars ribbons of fresh courgette. Add the dressing just before serving to preserve the crunchy texture. You can use any edible flowers to decorate, but borage — with its lovely pale blue, star-shaped flowers — is my favourite. Serve as a starter with crusty bread for mopping up the dressing.

To make the dressing, place the orange and lemon juice, salt, pepper and sugar in a bowl and whisk well. Add the olive oil and whisk again to emulsify and thicken the dressing. Taste and adjust seasoning if necessary.

To prepare the salad, use a potato peeler to make long, thin courgette ribbons, rotating around the courgette and discarding the softer centre. Place the ribbons in a bowl and toss with the herbs. Just before serving, pour over the salad dressing and mix, then garnish with the flowers.

Serves 4, as a side dish

5 medium-sized courgettes
Small handful of coriander leaves
Small handful of young mint leaves
Edible flowers, to garnish

For the dressing:
2 tablespoons freshly squeezed
   orange juice
1 tablespoon freshly squeezed
   lemon juice
½ teaspoon sea salt
Pinch of black pepper
Pinch of caster sugar
4 tablespoons extra-virgin olive oil

Daucus carota

CARROTS

It never wears off – the pure, dramatic pleasure of tugging up carrots. A gentle pull, a wobble to loosen, then the sudden release as the root slips out. They are a firm favourite with the children I work with.

Carrots are at their best when harvested sweet and finger-sized slender. At this smaller size, they are far superior to the chunky autumn carrots sold in shops. I like to grow carrots in deep containers or raised beds, filled with a light soil or compost. With this method, you can provide a perfect compost mix and avoid their main pest, the low-flying carrot root fly.

Carrot leaves are also edible, although often forgotten. Weirdly, in Britain there apparently was once a fashion for wearing decorative carrot fronds in the hair, like feathers.

Recommended varieties
Don't bother with fancy purple or yellow carrots. They look tempting but are trickier to grow, with disappointing yields. Stick with early and easily grown varieties such as 'Nantes' or 'Chantenay Red Cored', which is a tasty all-rounder. 'Parmex' and 'Paris Market Atlas' are rounder carrots that are well suited to containers. If carrot root fly is a problem, try modern varieties such as 'Flyaway'. Some companies sell varieties that are specifically grown for their young leaves.

Growing
The carrot itself is the main taproot, so unsurprisingly this plant hates being moved around. Sow in a sunny spot, directly where the carrots will grow. (It's possible to start them off in plug trays, but only if you transplant them extremely young, which is fiddly.)

Sow seed thinly from early spring to mid-summer. (Note that the seeds have a fine aroma.) Early crops, when the weather is still cold, are best with protection such as a layer of horticultural fleece – a fabric for protecting plants. Sow every three weeks for a steady supply. Thin out seedlings to avoid overcrowding – you won't get decent roots if the plants are squashed. *Spacing:* About 5cm between plants. Allow 15cm between rows.

Containers *Minimum compost depth:* 20cm. Carrots are ideal in deep containers and raised beds. Rounder varieties of carrot can thrive in more shallow containers. Aim for a light and free-draining compost mix. You want it low in nutrients, so do not add fertiliser, manure or similar. Adding handfuls of horticultural sharp sand to multipurpose compost will

roots, leaves

5/5

improve drainage and dilute nutrient levels. *Indoors:* This is possible, space permitting, but it may be easier to grow baby carrot leaves for salads as they require less container depth.

In the ground Carrots prefer a light and reasonably poor soil. Be wary if nutrient-rich manure has been added in the last year. If the soil is over-fertile you may end up with more leaf than root. The roots also struggle to grow downwards in heavy clay or stony soil. To prepare for sowing the fine seed, tug up any weeds and use a rake to break up or move aside any lumps of soil. If in doubt, grow in containers or raised beds or sow the rounder varieties of carrot.

Harvesting
The best method of storage is to leave carrots in the ground or container and harvest at the last moment. To ascertain carrot size before pulling, rub the soil or compost away from the top of the root to check the girth. Always pick carrot leaves for eating when small and tender.

Seed saving
Not straightforward. Carrots produce seed in the second year of their life cycle and varieties flowering nearby may cross-pollinate.

Pests and diseases
The main pest is carrot root fly. The insects fly low, attracted to the scent of carrot foliage, and lay eggs at the base of the plant. Larvae then tunnel into the roots. Carrots grown at ground level may be affected, but not on higher plots such as balconies and rooftops.

Symptoms include dead seedlings or stunted growth. Inspect roots for scars and tunnels. The simple solution is to grow carrots in a raised container, at least 60cm high. Alternatively, erect a solid physical barrier around your crop, using polythene or fine mesh, or grow plants beneath a layer of horticultural fleece or fine mesh, thoroughly tucked in around the edges. Always remove carrot thinnings as the scent attracts the flies. Some varieties of carrot offer a degree of resistance.

Preserving
Blanch and freeze chopped carrots or use in pickles and chutneys.

Notes
Carrots are in the Apiaceae family, also known as the umbels, which includes chervil, dill and coriander. These plants are biennials, with a two-year life cycle, although we eat the roots in their first year.

If you have spare room on your plot, leave a few plants in the ground over winter so that they produce spectacular flowers the following year. Beneficial insects will love them, too.

Try using carrots as a feathery edging on your plots.

5 WAYS WITH CARROTS

Enjoy your carrots when they are slender and small. I often eat mine raw. Roasting or steaming is the best way to cook them. You can boil, mash or grate carrots, but these methods are better suited to larger, shop-bought specimens. Carrot leaves are best eaten or used for decorating a plate when young. Carrots pair especially well with chervil, coriander, dill, fennel, parsley, cumin, cinnamon, star anise, caraway, ginger and orange.

* To roast carrots, toss with olive oil, sea salt and pepper, then cook, uncovered, in the oven at 200°C/400°F/gas 6 until they begin to crisp at the edges. For extra flavour, try adding rosemary, garlic, a splash of wine vinegar, a squeeze of orange juice and a pinch of cumin or other friendly spices.

* Serve up whole carrots as crudités. Try chilling them in the freezer for 5 minutes first for extra crunch, then serve with dips such as hummus, tsatsiki (see page 86) or tahini.

* Slowly fry baby carrots, sliced in half lengthways, in olive oil for 5–15 minutes, depending on size, or until turning golden. For a dressing, mix the carrots with freshly squeezed lemon and orange juice, mint and salt and pepper. This recipe is adapted from one in Sophie Grigson's excellent book *Vegetables*.

* For a luxurious side dish, slather steamed carrots in a creamy chervil sauce (see page 76).

* Don't waste the tiny carrots pulled when thinning out. Make a salad with the leaves and roots. Try them with coriander, shungiku, sliced radish and a sweet miso dressing (see page 122).

MAGIC CARROTS

This technique adds a magical extra dimension to your roots. It also works well with baby turnips and radishes. Serve with a light sprinkle of chopped chervil, chives, coriander or parsley.

Wash and trim the carrots, and slice any large specimens in half lengthways. Arrange them in a single layer in a shallow pan, skin-side up if sliced, with just enough water to cover. Add the butter, sugar, star anise and salt. Bring to the boil, then turn down the heat and cook, uncovered, at a vigorous simmer until the carrots are tender but not overcooked, and the liquid is thick and syrupy. Adjust the seasoning to taste and then flip the carrots to coat with the sauce. Serve with a sprinkle of green herbs.

Serves 2–4, as a side dish

300g whole young carrots (approx.)
Large knob of butter (approx. 20g)
1 tablespoon caster sugar
1 star anise
Pinch of salt
Chopped green herbs, to garnish

Melothria scabra

MOUSE MELONS

The mouse melon is an amazing plant, with many aliases: the children in my school garden call it a mini dragon's egg; botanists opt for the more pragmatic *Melothria scabra*. Other names include Mexican sour gherkin, cucamelon and pepquiño.

Whatever you call it, this ancient climbing plant is fun and easy to grow and makes the most of vertical space. It produces handfuls of bite-sized fruit with beautiful marbled skin and tastes like a crunchy cucumber with a refreshing hint of lemon. Mouse melons definitely have the wow factor, and are ace in kids' lunchboxes.

You may need to hunt around a bit online for the seeds. Mouse melons were rediscovered recently, having been cultivated in Mexico and Central America many centuries ago. I reckon they are destined to be a big hit with urban gardeners.

Recommended varieties A handful of suppliers sell the seed (see page 186). Search online under its various aliases and botanical name.

Growing Mouse melons need a sunny spot, at least one metre in height in which to climb and some method of support, as for peas (see page 48, but note that mouse melons climb higher than some pea varieties). The seed requires warmth to germinate, in the range of 17–20°c. Sow in mid-spring in a snug spot indoors. Alternatively, sow outdoors once the weather has warmed up in early summer. Sow in plug trays, two seeds per cell, or in small pots; once they have germinated, remove the weaker seedling. Harden off and plant out when the seedling has at least three sturdy leaves. *Spacing:* About 15cm between plants.

Containers *Minimum compost depth:* 20cm. Mouse melons can be grown in a deep container in the same way as peas (see page 49). As they are climbers, you could consider squeezing in some low-growing crops around the edge, such as radishes or lettuce. Use a general-purpose liquid feed, switching to a high-potassium feed once they start to flower and form fruit. *Indoors:* Tricky, as these are large climbing plants.

In the ground Mouse melons prefer a fertile soil. Prepare the planting hole as for courgettes (see page 37) and plant out hardened-off seedlings. Alternatively, sowing direct is possible if the soil is sufficiently warm.

fruit, flowers   4/5

Harvesting Mouse melons become sweeter as they ripen on the vine. Squeeze to gauge ripeness – a rock-hard fruit is not ready. Aim to harvest just before the vine drops the fruits.

Seed saving This is easy. Allow the fruits to ripen fully on the vine. Alternatively, pick up ripe fruit dropped by the plant. Transfer to a bright windowsill and leave for three more days. Cut in half, squeeze out the seeds, rinse, drain and dry thoroughly.

Pests and diseases Slugs may target seedlings, otherwise largely trouble-free.

Preserving Mouse melons are excellent in pickles (see overleaf).

Notes

Mouse melons are annuals in the Cucurbitaceae family, along with cucumbers, squashes and courgettes.

The vines can climb to around 2m in height, or you can brave the slugs and leave them to scramble over the ground if you have the space.

4 WAYS WITH MOUSE MELONS

Mouse melons are at their best raw. The tiny yellow flowers are also edible. They pair especially well with basil, coriander, dill, tomatoes, prawns and ginger.

❁ For a Mediterranean-style salad, mix mouse melons with cherry tomatoes, capers, basil and black olives. If you are keen for a dressing, keep it simple – just a few drops of vinegar and a sprinkle of sea salt.

❁ For a quick pickle, slice mouse melons in half lengthways, sprinkle with salt, mix well with your fingers, then leave in a colander for 15 minutes. Drain off any liquid and pat dry. For the pickle liquid, bring to the boil 50ml white wine vinegar and 2 teaspoons sugar. Stir to dissolve the sugar, then allow to cool. Pour over the mouse melons, mixing with plenty of dill.

❁ For a more oriental flavour, follow the process above, using 50ml rice wine vinegar and 2 teaspoons sugar. Once the liquid has cooled, add finely grated fresh ginger, a splash of light soy sauce and a few drops of sesame oil.

❁ Mix halved mouse melons with yoghurt, a pinch each of salt and caster sugar, plus mint or dill for a cooling Indian raita, to serve with curries.

DILL PICKLES

Makes 1 jar

200g mouse melons, or sufficient to fill jar
2 teaspoons sea salt
150ml cider vinegar or white wine vinegar
150ml water
10 black peppercorns
4 cloves
1 tablespoon brown sugar
3 dill sprigs, plus a few flowers if available

This is a mini-version of the ubiquitous dill pickle, popular from Warsaw to New York. They are a brilliant accompaniment to charcuterie, smoked fish and burgers. If available, add a sprig of dill flowers to the jar. You could spice up the pickling liquid with a chunk of bruised fresh ginger, coriander seeds, allspice or bay leaves.

Choose a sterilised jar (see page 184) that will snugly fit your mouse melons. Slice the mouse melons in half lengthways. Place in a colander and sprinkle with 1 teaspoon of the salt, mix with your fingers, then set aside for 20 minutes, slotting a bowl underneath the colander to collect the water that will drain off.

Bring the vinegar, water, spices, sugar and the second teaspoon of salt to the boil for 1 minute, then allow to cool. Taste the liquid, which should be both sweet and sour.

Pat dry the melons and fill the jar, adding the dill and dill flowers, if available. Pour over the pickling vinegar, taking care that it covers the mouse melons. Seal and store in the fridge.

Pisum sativum

PEAS

Peas reach for the sky, their finger-like tendrils gripping tightly as they climb. I find their gritty determination rather touching.

Try to make the most of their vertical habit: imagine a green wall of peas on your patio or balcony; or a thick hedge of pods to help mark out your plot.

For me, peas are mostly a garden snack. I grow mainly sugar snap and mangetout varieties, and often graze on them raw, when young and sweet. Pea shoots, the crunchy growing tips, are a brilliant crop and best grown separately, thickly sown into crates or seed trays. For me, peas in the pod are less of a priority, as shop-bought frozen peas are of terrific quality.

Recommended varieties There are three main types of pea. Carefully match them to your growing space, as they can reach to varying heights. Some traditional pea varieties, such as 'Alderman', can grow several metres tall so check before ordering.

Sugar snaps have round pods that can be eaten whole when young and tender. Try 'Delikett' or 'Sugar Ann'. Mangetouts such as 'Delikata' or 'Oregon Sugar Pod' have flatter pods and can also be eaten whole. Dwarf varieties suit container-growing and require less, if any, support. These include 'Kelvedon Wonder' and 'Markana', both of which produce peas in the pod. Popular heritage varieties include 'Purple Podded', which looks gorgeous, although the flavour is not as fine as that of many rivals.

For pea shoots, you can easily use dried peas from health-food shops – these are significantly cheaper.

Growing Peas are a cool-climate crop and prefer a sunny spot. A modest harvest is easy; a bumper crop takes a bit of skill. Choose varieties carefully and provide support as peas need many handholds. For shorter-growing varieties, the classic supports are pea sticks, which are just twigs or branches (traditionally cut from hazel or birch) pushed in along rows after sowing. For taller varieties, use netting or chicken wire stapled to trellis or stretched between upright poles 2m high. Alternatively, construct a wigwam with bamboo canes, winding string horizontally between the uprights.

Soaking pea seed overnight will hasten germination, but is not essential. Sow a first batch in early spring, then a second batch two to three months later. To be extra cunning, sow early, mid-season and late varieties each

fruit, shoots, flowers   3/5

time to extend your harvest. Also grow a few spares to fill any gaps.

Peas have especially deep roots, so shallow plug trays aren't ideal. It's better to sow three seeds into small pots or invest in root trainers, a type of extra-deep plug tray specifically designed to accommodate long roots. Plant out seedlings when about 10cm tall, watering well and mulching around the plants. You can also sow pea seed direct, for example in a zig zag, alternating seed either side of their support. *Spacing:* About 7cm between plants.

For pea shoots, sow seed very thickly into a seed tray or crate filled with multipurpose compost (see page 171). This method also works for growing the shoots of dried broad beans and black-eyed peas, among others.

Containers *Minimum compost depth:* 25cm. Peas have long roots, so grow in a deep container; pea shoots are less fussy in this respect. It is tricky to get a decent harvest of peas in a container, especially peas in the pod, so grow sugar snaps or mangetouts. Choose dwarf and compact varieties. Provide support, either in the form of a wigwam of bamboo canes or try growing taller varieties of peas up against an existing structure such as fencing or balcony railings. *Indoors:* Trays of pea shoots are most suitable.

In the ground Peas like a rich, moisture-retentive soil. Prepare the ground before planting if necessary. For example, you can improve a clay soil by digging in plenty of garden compost several weeks beforehand.

Harvesting Pick frequently, starting from the bottom of the plant. Avoid leaving mature pods. With secateurs or sharp fingernails, snip off at the knuckle, the junction where the pod joins the plant. Mangetouts and sugar snaps can be picked at any size. With pea shoots, snip off above the first leaves when around 5cm tall, and they should then regrow.

Seed saving This is easy as varieties rarely cross. Allow the pods to dry completely – they will turn brown on the plant and should rattle inside their pods. If the weather is wet, cut down the plant and further dry indoors.

Pests and diseases Birds can strip leaves – pea sticks or nets may help to deter them. Mice may eat the seed in open ground. Caterpillars inside pods indicate pea moth: try growing future crops under horticultural fleece or fine mesh, or switch to smaller mangetouts and sugar snaps, picking them when young. Powdery mildew often strikes peas at the end of their life cycle (see page 165).

Preserving Don't bother. When fresh supplies run out, turn to shop-bought frozen peas.

Notes

Peas are annuals in the Fabaceae family, also known as legumes, which includes broad beans and runner beans. Their flowers are self-pollinating, containing both male and female sex organs.

In general, water only when dry and increase watering once plants start to flower. Peas are susceptible to frost.

You can sow hardy varieties in autumn for a head start in spring, but it's worth the extra effort only if you are determined to get a super-early crop.

Above: Pea shoots, sown thickly and grown in a shallow container

10 WAYS WITH PEAS

Home-grown peas are often at their best eaten raw. I mainly cook with shop-bought peas from the freezer, where I also stash a bag of frozen edamame, those young soy beans they serve in Japanese restaurants, combining them two from time to time. Pea shoots are an everyday addition to salads. Pea flowers are pretty and edible, but harvest sparingly. Peas combine especially well with basil, dill, lemon verbena, mint, shiso, tarragon, bacon, chorizo, scallops, eggs, and cheeses such as feta or Parmesan.

Mangetouts and sugar snaps

❀ Keep it simple, and serve them raw in a bowl, perhaps with chunks of Parmesan to nibble or a yoghurt dip laced with plenty of chopped dill or mint.

❀ Steam for 2 minutes to soften slightly, then stir-fry with grated fresh ginger and sesame oil. Sprinkle with sesame seeds and light soy sauce, and serve. You could also add defrosted edamame.

❀ When cooking pasta, toss whole pods or shelled peas into the cooking water for the last minute or so, to mix into the dish.

❀ Chop and add to Vietnamese summer rolls (see page 88).

❀ Use mangetouts as a canapé base, with dollops of pesto or other toppings on top.

Peas in the pod

❀ Use as a canapé. Carefully open the pods, scoop out every other pea, and replace with small nuggets of feta cheese or diced chorizo. The pods then act as a serving dish, and you eat the peas raw.

❀ Make a pea purée to serve with roasted scallops or white fish. Blitz or mash a handful of cooked shelled peas with finely chopped mint, green shiso or basil. Then stir through a little cream, soured cream or yoghurt and season well, perhaps with a touch of nutmeg. Either serve chunky or push through a sieve for a finer consistency. This is equally good made with frozen peas. Warm the purée before serving.

Pea shoots

❀ Use liberally in salads, but avoid dousing in dressing, as their texture is best unadorned.

❀ Add to sandwiches, stir-fries and risottos.

❀ Include pea shoots in a mix for a pesto (see page 92).

'FEEL BETTER' BROTH

This is my favourite healing recipe, ideal after a heavy night out or if you are feeling under the weather. It is adapted from a recipe by Mayumi Nishimura in her book Mayumi's Kitchen. *Use any parts of the plant – I like including young pea pods and pea shoots. Alternatively, just use peas from the freezer. The other magic ingredient is dried wakame seaweed, also known as kelp. It's easy to find in health-food shops and Japanese grocers.*

In a pan, soak the wakame in the water for 10 minutes. Scoop out the seaweed, chop it roughly and return it to the pan. Bring the water to a gentle simmer. Add the onion and cook for 5 minutes. Add the pea pods and cook for a further 3 minutes, or until starting to soften. Add the ginger, soy sauce and white miso, simmer for a further 1 minute, then stir through the pea shoots. Taste, season with more soy if preferred, float a circle of chilli on the top, then serve.

Serves 1

6cm piece of wakame seaweed
  (approx. 10g)
300ml cold water
½ small onion, very finely sliced in strips
5 young pea pods, sliced on the
  diagonal if large
½ teaspoon grated fresh ginger
2 teaspoons light soy sauce
½ teaspoon white miso (optional)
Small handful of pea shoots
Slice of red chilli, to garnish

Dried wakame is sold whole, chopped into strips or as flakes. All will work in this recipe – simply use the quantity you prefer.

Raphanus sativus

RADISHES

I recently went for a swanky lunch in the Parisian restaurant L'Arpège. Three radishes were arranged on the tablecloth: a long, crimson root, shaped like a phallus; a rough, black specimen, like a grenade; and a small, round radish, cut in half to reveal delicate rose flesh encircled by vibrant green skin. Later, the chef Alain Passard sauntered over: 'Vegetable food is the best food for creativity, it's like a painting,' he said.

Radishes, in all their diversity, certainly provide the most wonderful palette. They are swift and easy to grow, and the roots, leaves and flowers are all edible. The young seedpods also make a spicy snack.

For some reason, radishes are not much appreciated in the west. Look east, however, and they are held in great esteem. It is said that the Chinese have cultivated radishes since 3000BC.

Recommended varieties Breakfast radishes, the standard round type, are the quickest and easiest to grow. Try 'Cherry Belle', 'Sparkler' and 'Amethyst', which is a lovely deep purple; 'French Breakfast' is more tapered in shape; 'White Icicle' has tasty white flesh; 'München Bier' is the variety to grow for its seedpods.

Oriental radishes include stunning bicoloured varieties such as 'Red Flesh' and the huge mooli-type radishes, also known as daikon in Japan. Winter radishes are hardier and take two months or more to mature. Recommended varieties include 'China Rose'. Most should be sown after mid-summer.

Growing Radishes grow very quickly, with some maturing in less than a month. Sow seed thinly direct in their final positions. Most varieties can be sown from early spring until late summer. Choose a spot with decent sun except in the hottest months, when they prefer partial shade. Water the site beforehand and sow every few weeks for a constant supply. Thin out seedlings if cramped. *Spacing:* From about 7cm for small radishes to 20cm for larger types. Allow 15cm between rows.

Containers *Minimum compost depth:* 10cm for small radishes, up to 40cm for large and long mooli types. Use any multipurpose compost and keep it moist. Consider sowing a mix of varieties in one container. Pop radishes in around other plants to fill any gaps. *Indoors:* Radishes are a useful and quick crop in shallow containers.

roots,
seed pods,
leaves,
flowers

4/5

In the ground Radishes thrive in a light soil that is rich, weed-free and moisture-retentive. Improve clay soils by digging in garden compost or similar before sowing. If growing long radishes, such as the mooli varieties, prepare the soil to a greater depth, around 40cm.

Harvesting Pull promptly, when juicy and crunchy, as radishes peak for just a week or two. Pungency increases in hot weather. When picking the pods, taste as you go – the best are young and crisp.

Seed saving It's easy to collect seed from the dried seedpods, but be aware that nearby varieties may have cross-pollinated with your plants.

Pests and diseases Slugs and snails may target seedlings. Holes in the leaves indicate flea beetle: the plants will still be edible, but grow them under horticultural fleece if this is a concern.

Preserving Radishes are terrific in quick pickles.

Notes

Radishes are annuals and biennials in the Brassicaceae (brassica) family, also known as the crucifers, which includes mustards, cabbages and kales.

Quick-growing radishes are useful for filling in bare patches on the plot. Dot them around and sow among slower-growing crops.

Water regularly, as the roots turn unpleasantly hot and woody if the soil becomes dry. Hot weather may also cause them to bolt, prematurely running to flower.

7 WAYS WITH RADISHES

Radishes are beautiful left whole, but it's also fun to mix up the textures by chopping the roots into halves, quarters or eighths, or slicing them paper-thin. Show off the colours of different varieties. The young leaves can be eaten raw and whole; hairier large leaves are best shredded, liquidised or gently braised to soften. When available, radish flowers add a decorative flourish and have good flavour. The spicy, juicy seedpods are delicious when young, before they go woody. Radishes pair especially well with coriander, dill, mint, apple, orange, lemon and salt.

❁ Serve the roots French style, with a dish each of soft butter and sea salt, dipping from one to the other. Add seedpods too, if to hand.

❁ Create a quick salad by slicing the roots into quarters lengthways and mixing them with strips of apple, mint and a salad dressing made with cider vinegar, wholegrain mustard and cold-pressed rapeseed oil. A few pomegranate seeds add colour and a sweet, juicy crunch.

❁ Add the leaves to salads when small. Alternatively, sauté fresh ginger, garlic and chilli until soft, add the leaves and a squeeze of citrus juice and cook until wilted. I like serving this on toast, such as bruschetta, with goat's cheese or mozzarella.

❁ Cook the leaves in the same way as beetroot leaves. Try combining them with raisins and pine nuts (see page 22).

❁ Use the leaves in recipes for watercress soup and serve with a dollop of crème fraîche or yoghurt.

❁ Offer the seedpods as a crunchy snack with evening drinks or add to vegetable mixes for pickles.

❁ Add chunks of winter radish to slow-cooked dishes such as stews.

Above centre: A harvest of mooli radish

INSTANT RADISH PICKLE

*One of my big discoveries this year has been Japanese-style instant pickles
– a brilliant way of adding texture and flavour (see page 182). This recipe stars
radishes, but you could also add thin slices of carrot, baby turnip, beetroot
and cabbage. Lemon slices or green shiso leaves will further lift the flavour.
Serve as a palate cleanser with Asian food.*

Wash the radishes and twist off the leaves. Blanch the leaves by dunking
them in boiling water for 1 minute. Refresh by plunging in iced water and
drain. Squeeze between your hands to remove as much water as possible.
Chop as you like and place in a bowl or plastic container.

Slice the radish roots into eighths or 5mm slices. Deseed and finely chop
the chilli. Combine both with the chopped leaves and salt, mixing well with
your fingers. Leave for about 2 hours, preferably weighted down to press
out water to drain off later. (I place a saucer on top of the radishes in the
bowl, weighing it down with a heavy teapot.)

Drain off the water, rinse off excess salt, and again squeeze out the
remaining moisture with your hands. Return to the container with
any flavourings you wish to add, such as slices of lemon or torn green
shiso leaves.

To serve, arrange the pickles in a small bowl. Season with a few drops of
toasted sesame oil, mirin or soy sauce, if you like.

Serves 4, as a small side dish

1 bunch of radishes (approx. 200g),
  including leaves
1 dried red chilli, soaked in warm water
1 teaspoon sea salt (4g or 2% of radish
  weight)
Lemon slices or shiso leaves (optional)
Toasted sesame oil, mirin and/or sesame
  seeds (optional)

Solanum lycopersicum

TOMATOES

Tomatoes are a classic home-grown crop, but demand sun and attention. Grow them if you are blessed with a sunny spot, indoors or outdoors, that receives at least six hours of direct sunlight per day.

The prize is a fully ripe tomato with thin skin and full flavour – far superior to the travesties in shops. My mate Mark often manages six kilos per plant, from craggy red beefsteaks to tiny yellow cherry tomatoes.

I daydream of the glasshouses of aristocrat Louis Albert de Broglie, known as 'Le Prince Jardinier' ('Prince Gardener'), who grows 650 varieties at his château in France.

Recommended varieties Centuries of breeding have created a vast choice, including cherry, standard, plum and beefsteak types. Varieties generally suit either indoor or outdoor growing, so choose accordingly.

If you can't offer plenty of sun, grow varieties that produce smaller fruit. Cherry and baby plum tomatoes, for example, ripen far more quickly than a large beefsteak. 'Sungold', 'Sakura', 'Rosada' and 'Apero' are all fine examples and F1 hybrids (see page 176).

In general, tomatoes are grouped loosely as either 'determinates' (commonly known as 'bush') or 'indeterminates' ('cordon' or 'vine'). Bush tomatoes stop growing at a certain, determined size to produce maximum fruit over a short period. This makes them ideal for container-growing. 'Maskotka' and 'Tumbling Tom' or 'Tumbler' are cherry tomatoes well suited to window boxes and hanging baskets.

Cordon tomatoes will continue growing and crop more heavily over a longer period. They require more care, such as support, pruning and 'stopping' (see notes opposite). 'Gardener's Delight' is a recommended cordon tomato and grows well in containers. 'Ailsa Craig' ripens early with fine flavour. Heritage varieties are open-pollinated and therefore suitable for providing seed to save (see opposite). Choose varieties that suit your climate. You may also find modern grafted tomatoes, where the fruiting vine is melded to a rootstock. These can be high quality but are pricey.

Growing Grow from seed in early to mid-spring, or buy plants later in the season. Sow two seeds per small pot and place in a warm spot indoors, such as a windowsill, at around 20°c. Remove the weaker plant at seedling stage.

fruit   5/5

Pot on seedlings whenever they outgrow their current pot. Check by sliding the plant out to see if the roots are becoming restricted. Transfer to a pot with a slightly larger diameter, with fresh compost. Plant tomatoes more deeply each time you move them, as they can grow new roots from the lower section of their stem. *Spacing:* Depends on variety; typically 50cm between plants.

Containers *Minimum compost depth:* 20cm. Choose suitable varieties. Mix a slow-release fertiliser into the compost mix. Use a general-purpose liquid feed as they grow, switching to a high-potassium feed once they start to flower and form fruit. *Indoors:* Suitable varieties will thrive in a sunny indoor spot. When they start to flower, assist pollination by gently shaking the plants to loosen pollen and help the flowers to set fruit.

In the ground Harden off young plants (see page 16) and plant out in early summer, once all risk of frost has passed. Mix a slow-release fertiliser into the planting hole beforehand.

Harvesting
Pick ripe on the vine, ideally still warm from the sun. Avoid watering beforehand to intensify flavour. Store at room temperature. To help ripen green tomatoes, place them in a paper bag with a ripe banana.

Seed saving
This is relatively easy. Harvest over-ripe tomatoes, then scoop the seeds into a sterile jar half-filled with lukewarm water. Leave, loosely covered, for three days, swirling occasionally. The mixture will slightly ferment. Scoop off the surface debris, rinse the seeds with fresh water and place them on paper out of direct sun. Leave to dry for about ten days, turning daily. Tomato seed is viable for at least five years.

Pests and diseases
Slugs may target seedlings. The main menace is blight, a dramatic affliction that can devastate plants late in the season. Symptoms are a sudden shrivelling and rotting of leaves and fruit. There is no easy cure, although indoor-grown plants are less susceptible and some modern varieties promise a degree of resistance. Dispose of infected plants and do not add to a compost heap. Rots on the bottom of fruits are often the results of irregular watering. Tomatoes grown under glass may be affected by red spider mite, whitefly and aphids (see pages 163 and 165).

Preserving
For unripe fruit, green tomato chutney is the classic preserve. For very ripe tomatoes, you could make passata, an Italian tomato sauce suitable for freezing. To dry tomatoes, cut in half, place on a roasting tray, cut side facing upwards, sprinkle with olive oil, salt, a little sugar, thyme or rosemary and leave them in the lowest possible oven overnight. When they are cool, place them in a jar, cover with olive oil and store in the fridge.

Notes

Tomatoes are half-hardy annuals in the Solanaceae family, which includes chillies, potatoes and aubergines. Avoid growing tomatoes next to these crops or in spots where blight struck the previous season.

Tomatoes are self-fertile as the flowers contain both male and female organs. However, indoor-grown tomatoes may need help with pollination (see left).

It helps to understand the plant's natural habit. In the wild, tomatoes are straggly vines producing abundant leaves and small fruit. Our job is to bend the plants ruthlessly to our will, coaxing them to form more fruit and less leaf – this typically involves tying them to stakes and nipping out excess shoots.

Always give tomatoes a good soak when watering as they have deep roots.

With cordon tomatoes, snip out side shoots as they grow. You can pot up these cuttings for new plants. You should also 'stop' cordon tomatoes by pinching out the growing tip in late summer once the plant is of sufficient size or has six trusses or clusters of ripening fruit.

Tomato plants may need support, especially cordon types. Tie them to thick bamboo canes, spiral stakes or similar. Alternatively, if growing indoors, you could suspend string from the ceiling, fasten it to the base of the plant and twist in the tomato stem as it grows.

Once the bottom leaves start to turn yellow, remove them up to the lowest cluster of fruit.

7 WAYS WITH TOMATOES

Use tomatoes at room temperature for full flavour. Mix them up with an array of colours and tastes. It's occasionally worth peeling off the skin and deseeding tomatoes, for example for salsas or sauces. With a sharp knife, score the skin with a cross at the bottom of the fruit, place in a bowl and cover with boiling water. Scoop out 10–20 seconds later, depending on size, drop into cold water, peel off the skin, slice and scoop out the seeds – a teaspoon is handy for this. Tomatoes pair especially well with basil, coriander, parsley, garlic, avocado, capers, anchovies, bacon and olives.

❀ For the most simple of pleasures, make *Pan con Tomate*, the Spanish staple. Cut in half ripe tomatoes and a peeled garlic clove. Toast some good-quality bread (sourdough is best), rub with the garlic, then rub in the tomatoes to release their lovely juices (discard the skin). Drizzle with olive oil and season with salt and pepper.

❀ Try Piedmontese Peppers, a brilliantly simple light lunch or starter. Preheat your oven to 200°C/400°F/gas 6. Carefully chop a red pepper in half lengthways, through the stalk, then cut out the white flesh and shake out the seeds; sprinkle the cavity with pepper and a little salt, then add halved tomatoes (or whole cherry tomatoes) and thin slivers of garlic and anchovy; cover with a tablespoon of the best olive oil and bake in an oiled shallow roasting tray for around 40 minutes. Eat when cool, with a basil leaf on top.

❀ For a simple salad to show off your tomato harvest, arrange a large plate with interlapping tomato slices of different colours, then sprinkle with fresh herbs and sea salt.

❀ Try a peach, tomato and basil salad, a brilliant combination from chef Rowley Leigh. Dress with lemon juice, oil, pepper and basil leaves.

❀ Dice for a tomato salsa (see page 31), or whizz up a Spanish gazpacho.

❀ For something special, slow-roast whole cherry tomatoes until soft and squidgy – this technique gives them a unique texture and intensity. Carefully peel off the skin (see above), sprinkle with caster sugar and cook in an oven at 110°C/225°F/gas ¼ for 1–1½ hours. These are fantastic with mozzarella or burrata cheese (see page 28).

❀ For fried green tomatoes, dip into a beaten egg followed by a batter of polenta maize or flour, then fry until crisp. Serve with a tahini dressing (see page 23) or aioli (see page 155).

TOMATO & LEMONGRASS RASAM

In India, chef Hemant Oberoi is a big cheese — a famous avant-garde chef, known for modern twists on traditional dishes. This recipe is inspired by his aromatic take on the traditional rasam, a wonderful light soup from southern India. Serve as an appetiser before a dinner or as lunch with basmati rice.

I first tried Hemant's version at a chilli-themed meal, where the chef shared tales of dusty recipes he'd discovered, including a Tamil dish for newlyweds of a spiced meatball sewn into a banana leaf. The couple pulled either end of the thread and whoever caught the meatball was destined to be the dominant one in the marriage.

Rinse the lentils in cold water, drain and then place in a large saucepan with 1 litre of cold water, one of the lemongrass stalks and the turmeric. Bring to the boil, then reduce the heat and simmer, uncovered, for 20 minutes, or until the lentils are tender. Discard the lemongrass stalk, but do not drain. Use a stick blender or liquidiser to blitz the lentils in the cooking water, then set aside.

In a second saucepan, of similar size, heat the vegetable oil and add the ginger, garlic, peppercorns, second lemongrass stalk, tomatoes and the coriander, including the stalks but keeping back a few leaves for the garnish. Cook for half a minute or so, stirring regularly.

Take the reserved lentil water, give it a stir, then strain in this liquid, discarding any sediment left in the sieve. (I often snack on it later). Rinse out the lentil pan.

Simmer the rasam for 10 minutes, covered, or until the tomatoes are soft and cooked. Strain the rasam back into the rinsed lentil pan. Push any tomato pulp through the sieve and scrape this in, too. Aim to be left with just tomato skins and other aromatics in the sieve, which you can now discard.

Tasting as you go, adjust the seasoning by adding the tamarind or lime juice, salt and sugar. Before serving, heat the vegetable oil for the extra spices in a small frying pan and add the mustard and cumin seeds. When the mustard seeds start to crackle, pour the spices into the rasam, stir vigorously, then serve, garnishing each bowl with a coriander leaf.

Serves 4, as an appetiser, or 2, as part of a main meal

60g yellow, pink or red lentils
2 lemongrass stalks, sliced in half lengthways
½ teaspoon turmeric
1 teaspoon vegetable oil
10g piece of fresh ginger, peeled and roughly crushed
2 garlic cloves, crushed
8 peppercorns
5 ripe medium-sized tomatoes, roughly chopped
Handful of coriander, including stalks
½ teaspoon tamarind paste (or substitute with a squeeze of lime juice)
Pinch of salt
Pinch of brown sugar

For the extra spices:
1 teaspoon vegetable oil
¼ teaspoon mustard seeds
¼ teaspoon cumin seeds

A recycled bathtub, planted with
lettuce, coriander and chervil

HERBS

62 **CHIVES**

66 **LEMON VERBENA**

70 **DILL**

74 **CHERVIL**

78 **CORIANDER**

84 **MINT**

90 **BASIL**

96 **SHISO**

100 **SORREL**

104 **THYME**

Culinary herbs are typically plants with a strong flavour added to food in modest quantities. So they are lumped together by their pungency and use in the kitchen, although these are matters of taste and habit rather than a botanical distinction. A Lebanese tabbouleh salad, for example, is made with handfuls of parsley, used more like a salad leaf.

I think it's more helpful to distinguish between 'soft' and 'hard' herbs. Basil, chervil, coriander, dill, mint and shiso are examples with softer leaves, best eaten raw or added at the end of cooking to retain their vibrant character. Don't forget to use their flavoursome stalks, too.

Thyme and rosemary, however, have tougher, woody stems with more robust, fibrous leaves. Add whole sprigs early to a dish to infuse their flavour, then fish them out before serving. Or finely chop the leaves.

In this section, you will find my favourite herbs. If you have the space, squeeze in others such as parsley, rosemary, tarragon, lovage, marjoram, sage and both summer and winter savory.

Supermarkets now sell a limited range of potted herbs. Designed to be harvested swiftly, these are often grown quickly with extra light and nutrients, so are weak and flimsy with a less intense flavour. Harden them off before attempting to grow them outdoors (see page 16). You can also try separating the seedlings and then planting the strongest in separate pots.

Allium schoenoprasum. A. tuberosum

CHIVES

Chives make your food look beautiful. I would still grow them even if they tasted of dishwater. The emerald-green leaves are unusual – tubular and upright. The pom-pom flowers dazzle in purples and pinks.

On the plot, they are easily grown perennials excellent for edging, dividing and dotting around in clumps. In the kitchen, chives add a flourish of colour and geometrical shape: snip the leaves into small rings or arrange whole in straight lines. Sprinkle the tiny, pink petals as a flourish.

Recommended varieties Common chives are your best bet. You may find a dozen or so varieties, such as 'Pink Perfection', but these are more decorative than edible. Garlic chives are a distinct species and well worth growing. These have flat, grass-like leaves with a more garlicky flavour, and bear pretty, white flowers later in the season.

Growing Chives prefer a rich soil and will tolerate light shade. You can grow from seed, but note that it may take up to six months to get a decent clump. Sow in plug trays in early spring, around five seeds per cell, or direct into their final position.

A quicker and easier option is to beg or buy established plants. Ask a friend to divide and slice you off a clump of chives (see opposite), or buy a pot from the supermarket or garden centre. Plant about five bulbs together, which will swiftly grow into a larger clump. *Spacing:* About 20cm between clumps.

Containers *Minimum compost depth:* 20cm. Chives spread quickly, so containers help keep them in check. The plants have deep roots so choose a suitable pot. Chives enjoy a rich, soil-based compost mix.

Water regularly, taking care that the roots do not dry out. Use a general-purpose liquid feed. Consider planting chives around the edge of a container, leaving the middle for plants with a contrasting leaf shape, such as tomatoes or carrots. *Indoors:* A pot of chives on the kitchen windowsill is useful for instant garnishes.

In the ground Choose your spot carefully, as a chive patch is a permanent feature. The herb is useful for spots with a touch of shade. Plant out bulbs or sprinkle seed and wait. Chives will die back during the winter. To extend the season, divide your clump and pot them up into a container to take indoors.

leaves, flowers | 5/5

Harvesting An established clump can be harvested several times during a season and will regrow remarkably quickly. Snip off whole leaves as required, 5cm above ground level. You could also use flowering chives as cut flowers.

Propagation Chives grow swiftly so you can divide the clumps every few years in spring or autumn. Use a spade or trowel to dig through the roots, replanting half of the chives elsewhere and leaving the original clump to grow on. You can also save their dried seed after they have flowered.

Pests and diseases Largely trouble-free.

Preserving Snip individual portions of the leaves into an ice-cube tray, without water, then freeze. Or use the leaves in a herb butter (see page 182). You can also dry the flowers.

Notes

Chives are hardy herbaceous perennials in the Liliaceae family, grouped with onions, leeks and garlic in the Allium genus.

The flowers are attractive to pollinating insects.

7 WAYS WITH CHIVES

Common chives are best cut with scissors into lengths and rings. Garlic chives, with their flat leaves, have less artistic potential. Add chive leaves at the end of any cooking. The flowers have a mild onion flavour. Harvest flowers when young, before they become too dry and papery, then snip individual florets from the flower head. Chives pair especially well with mint, beetroot, ginger, cheese, tomatoes, potatoes and eggs.

✿ Use the pinkish flowers to bring colour to a plate, for example by sprinkling florets over rice dishes or using whole flower heads to crown a bowl of magnificent salad or pasta.

✿ Use whole chives to create visual effects when decorating a plate, arranging in squares and triangles to frame your food.

✿ Snip the vibrant green leaves into dishes such as potato salads, salads, scrambled eggs, omelettes or soups.

✿ Cook up a batch of clapshot, a Scottish twist on mashed potatoes. Boil equal quantities of potatoes and swede or turnip, then mash with plenty of butter and stir through chopped chives. Season well with salt and pepper.

✿ Toss garlic chives into stir fries, adding at the end of the cooking to maintain their texture.

✿ Mix chives into soft cheeses, crème fraîche or soured cream, seasoning with lemon juice, salt and pepper to taste. Use as a dip or add a melting dollop to a baked potato.

✿ Wrap chives into Vietnamese summer rolls (see page 88) or Korean-style wraps (see page 122).

Aloysia citriodora
LEMON VERBENA

Fragrant beyond words, lemon verbena stirs up childhood memories of sticky lemon sherbets. The leaves, and their gorgeous essential oils, have long been cherished by chemists. For the home-grower it's a brilliant herb for sorbets, cocktails, salads and enlivening the senses.

Lemon verbena is a delicate plant which shudders from the cold but will live for years if treated with care. It is best grown in containers, then moved indoors during winter, when it will drop its leaves and hibernate.

I grow it as part of my 'tea patch', a group of herbs that brew up lovely infusions. It's also a multi-sensory favourite with kids – they love rubbing the leaves and sniffing their lemony fingers. Note that this plant is often confused with the distinctly different lemon balm (*Melissa officinalis*), which has serrated, softer leaves.

Recommended varieties There is unlikely to be a choice.

Growing Buy an established plant from a herb nursery or pinch a cutting from friends. Choose your sunniest spot and decide if you will risk growing the plant in the ground or play safe in a moveable container. *Spacing:* About ½m between plants.

Containers *Minimum compost depth:* 20cm. Create a light, free-draining compost mix. To improve drainage, add handfuls of horticultural sharp sand or grit. Use a general-purpose liquid feed. Move outdoor plants inside during the winter months. If they must stay outdoors when the temperature drops, wrap the container in bubble wrap and cover the plant with a protective layer of horticultural fleece. *Indoors:* In a sunny spot this is the best place for the herb, especially during cold weather.

Refresh the compost every spring: carefully tip the plant out of its container, scrape off any loose compost, then move into a slightly larger pot, filling with fresh compost.

In the ground Lemon verbena prefers a light and very well-drained soil in full sun with shelter. If in doubt, grow in a container.

Harvesting Try to pinch out the growing tips when you harvest the leaves, as this encourages a bushy plant (see page 17).

leaves, flowers — 5/5

Propagation Raise new plants from cuttings taken in spring or summer (see page 178).

Pests and diseases Largely trouble-free.

Preserving Dried leaves will retain some aroma and flavour. Alternatively, whizz the leaves with caster sugar in a food processor and freeze.

Notes

Lemon verbena is a half-hardy, deciduous perennial shrub in the Verbenaceae family, native to South and North America. It may drop its leaves in winter but will bounce back in spring.

The plant can be rather straggly, so trim as you harvest and prune in spring, cutting back any dead or untidy growth from last year.

6 WAYS WITH LEMON VERBENA

Eat young leaves whole or chopped. Larger leaves and whole sprigs are useful for infusing flavour, for example in sugar syrups. The tiny flowers are a rare edible treat. The herb pairs especially well with mint, carrots, currants, apples and fish.

❀ For a simple and soothing herb tea, soak the leaves in hot water. The French call this a *tisane de vervaine*. Try in combination with mint, too. Or add lemon verbena leaves to black tea for a lemony edge.

❀ Add young leaves to salads or wrap into Vietnamese summer rolls (see page 88) or Korean-style wraps (see page 122).

❀ Pair lemon verbena with fruit, adding the leaves to compotes, fruit salads and summer puddings.

❀ Mix the leaves into a salt cure for home-curing mackerel or salmon (see page 73).

❀ Infuse lemon verbena into sugar syrups and custards for jellies, cakes and tarts.

❀ Add the leaves to a fingerbowl of warm water when scoffing messy food with your fingers.

HERB-INFUSED CHOCOLATE GANACHE

Makes icing sufficient for a medium-sized cake or about 40 truffles

35g lemon verbena leaves
100g golden caster sugar
300ml water
350g dark chocolate, broken into pieces

This is a simple technique for flavouring chocolate with herbs. The recipe is adapted from a version that uses mint in chocolatier Paul A. Young's book Adventures with Chocolate. *As he explains, a ganache is a melted emulsion of chocolate and cream, or, in this case, water. You can use it while it is warm to ice a cake or when cooled to make truffles (see page 82). This recipe also works especially well with mint, green and purple shiso or basil.*

Tear the verbena leaves to release their natural oils. Place the sugar in a pan with the water, bring to the boil, add the lemon verbena leaves and simmer for 3 minutes, then allow to cool completely. Strain the mixture, bring it back to a simmer, then pour it over the chocolate, whisking well until smooth. Allow to cool for around 30 minutes before using.

GIN SMASH

If I were filthy rich, I would fill my shelves with first-edition, leather-bound books. First up would be Vilmorin-Andrieux's The Vegetable Garden *(1885). Second,* Cooling Cups and Dainty Drinks *(1869), by a chap called William Terrington. This cocktail is inspired by the latter. It was first made for me by my friend and drinks guru Dez O'Connell.*

Equip yourself with a cocktail shaker and a batch of sugar syrup – this is dead easy to make and provides a consistent drink. This recipe is for one person, so scale up as necessary.

To make the sugar syrup, place the sugar and water in a saucepan and warm gently. Stir continuously, well below boiling point, until all the sugar has dissolved. Allow the mixture to cool, then fine-strain into a sealable container. Store in the fridge, where it should keep for 2 weeks. Discard if it becomes cloudy or streaky.

To make the cocktail, first chill your glass. Fill with ice cubes and set aside.

Shake all the ingredients hard with ice and 2 teaspoons of the the sugar syrup in a cocktail shaker. Tip out the ice from the chilled glass, then strain in the cocktail. Garnish with a twist of orange zest.

Serves 1

Ice cubes
60ml London dry gin (Tanqueray, Beefeater or Citadelle are decent brands)
10 lemon verbena leaves
8 mint leaves
Large strip of orange zest

For the sugar syrup:
200g granulated sugar
100ml water

A standard sugar syrup for cocktails is made with two parts sugar to one part water. So you can adjust the quantities above as needed. A quick way to measure is to use a cup.

Anethum graveolens

DILL

Dill has a distinct flavour and character, and is a classic herb in the Nordic and Eastern European kitchen – think home-cured gravlax, subtle sauces and classy pickles. Just a few fronds bring a dish to life, and I'm on a mission to use every day.

The delicate plant is also popular in Laos and Iran, where it stars in several fish dishes. A quick suggestion – have a sniff when you tear open the seed packet. Even the seed has a divine fragrance.

Recommended varieties There is not a wide choice. You may find 'Dukat', which produces high-quality leaves.

Growing Dill prefers a sunny, well-drained spot. If in doubt, improve drainage by adding handfuls of grit. You can start the seed off early indoors at the beginning of spring; sow in plug trays, about three seeds per cell, and plant out as a small clump. Alternatively, sow in mid-spring, directly where the plant will grow. Sow every three weeks until late summer for a steady supply. Use a general-purpose liquid feed. *Spacing:* About 20cm between plants.

Containers *Minimum compost depth:* 20cm. It's best to use a deep container, although if you are growing small plants you can get away with something more shallow. Ideally, add handfuls of grit to your compost mix to improve drainage, and keep well watered. Sow seed direct into your container or start them off in plug trays first. *Indoors:* A pot of dill is handy on a kitchen windowsill, but won't last long. If possible grow in bulk outdoors.

In the ground Choose a suitable spot and sow direct. Aim to establish a self-seeding patch that will look after itself. If the seed fails to germinate in one spot, try another.

Harvesting Dill is a cut-and-come-again crop, so pick off the larger leaves, allowing the smaller leaves to grow on.

Seed saving This is relatively easy. In the right conditions, plants sown in spring and grown outdoors should flower and set seed. Chop off the flower heads when the seed is brown and dry, and dry for a further week indoors. Alternatively, allow the plant to self-seed.

leaves, seeds · 5/5

Pests and diseases Largely trouble-free.

Preserving Dill leaves will freeze whole, although they lose flavour and texture. I prefer adding the leaves to a herb butter (see page 182). Use dill flowers and seeds to flavour pickles.

Notes

Dill is a hardy annual in the Apiaceae family, also known as the umbels, which includes carrots and chervil. It can cope with low temperatures so is a good choice over winter.

Don't dig up and move the plant, as dill dislikes disturbance.

Keep well watered, especially during spells of hot weather.

If growing plants outdoors, allow a few to flower. The flower heads are beautiful in their own right and much enjoyed by insects such as bees and hoverflies.

6 WAYS WITH DILL

Dill is delicate so try not to overwhelm the herb with other strong flavours. The leaf, flower heads and seeds are all edible. Add dill leaves at the end of cooking to retain their flavour. Dill pairs especially well with mint, beetroot, cucumber, eggs, mushrooms, peas and seafood.

* Make your own Indian raita by adding dill leaves and chopped cucumber to plain yoghurt, with a pinch of salt and caster sugar.
* Mix dill into mayonnaise or into soured cream as a topping for blinis, adding lemon zest and a squeeze of lemon juice.
* For a whole-fish dish with Laotian flavours, make a fragrant stuffing: blitz a handful of dill leaves in a food processor with a stalk of lemongrass, a shallot, a clove of garlic and a couple of kaffir lime leaves, then stuff into the belly of the gutted fish, wrap in foil and bake. This works especially well with sea bream and sea bass.
* Stir the fragrant leaves through dishes of peas, broad beans or creamy mashed potato.
* Add a generous amount of dill to a white sauce for a fish pie, plus a splash of white wine and a pinch of white sugar.
* Use dill in cucumber pickles (see pages 46).

HOME-CURED MACKEREL

As a city boy, I was never taken out fishing. Later, I felt mildly embarrassed. After all, what kind of bloke has never caught a fish? So I got myself a sea kayak and proudly caught my first the other day – a juicy fat mackerel.

This recipe is based on the classic Nordic gravlax, but uses mackerel instead of salmon (the 'lax'). It's very simple to prepare. Dill is the traditional herb, but green shiso also works well.

Start the process at least a day before serving, to allow the cure to firm up and flavour the fish. Make the effort to buy (or catch) extremely fresh mackerel, asking the fishmonger to remove any bones from the fillets. The cured mackerel will keep in the fridge for a week or will freeze.

Cut a large square of cling film, sufficient to wrap the fillets in a stack, and lay flat on a plate. In a bowl, mix together the sugar, salt, pepper and dill for the mackerel cure. Roughly divide this cure mixture into five, for even distribution over the fillets.

Start to assemble alternating layers of cure and mackerel. Place one portion of cure in the centre of the cling film, then press a fillet on top, skin-side down, spreading the cure evenly beneath. Sprinkle a second portion of cure over the fillet flesh, then press another fillet on top, flesh-side down. You should now have a mackerel and dill sandwich. Sprinkle the third portion of cure on the skin, then repeat the process with the third and fourth fillets until you have a stack of the two fish. Top with the final portion of cure.

Wrap tightly in the cling film, then use another layer of cling film to double wrap. Place in a bowl or container, then refrigerate for at least a day, preferably two.

To serve, carefully unwrap the fillets over the sink, allowing the juices to drain away. Brush off the cure and pat dry the mackerel. If you want to remove the skin before serving, place the fillets skin-side down on a chopping board and carefully slide a sharp knife between the skin and flesh. Alternatively, just peel off the thin and more translucent outer layer of the mackerel skin, then slice the flesh into slivers

To make the sauce, mix together the mustard, honey and vinegar, whisk in the oil, then add the dill. Or whizz all the ingredients together in a blender or food processor. Serve with the mackerel and some bread.

Serves 4, as a starter

For the mackerel cure:
25g golden caster sugar
20g sea salt
½ teaspoon freshly ground black pepper
Handful of chopped dill leaves (about 10g)
4 large mackerel fillets (skin on, bones removed)

For the honey mustard sauce:
1 tablespoon mustard (English or Dijon)
1 tablespoon honey
1 tablespoon white wine vinegar
3 tablespoons vegetable oil
2 tablespoons chopped dill leaves

Anthriscus cerefolium
CHERVIL

Chervil is a classy ingredient that chefs like to keep for themselves – restaurant suppliers sell it but our shops don't. So chefs use the herb to lend a fancy and exclusive flourish to their menus.

Well, it's time to fight back and cook at home with chervil too. This is a delicate, fine herb with a beguiling and subtle taste – a hint of aniseed and parsley, which is particularly excellent with white fish.

The plant is easy to grow, puts up with some shade and can last well into winter. Establish a chervil patch and grow in bulk for a steady stash.

Recommended varieties There is not a wide choice; some may offer more curly leaves.

Growing Sow from spring to early autumn. Late-summer sowings are often the most successful. Choose a cool, moist spot with a touch of shade. The seed is slow to germinate, so be patient. Sow direct where it is to grow, every month for a steady supply, and thin at seedling stage if cramped. Alternatively, sow in plug trays, four seeds per cell to form a clump, and plant out as seedlings. *Spacing:* About 20cm between plants.

Containers *Minimum compost depth:* 10cm. Use multipurpose compost in wide, shallow containers to maximise growing area. I use recycled plastic vegetable trays (see page 171). Use a general-purpose liquid feed. *Indoors:* Chervil does fine indoors in a cool spot. Try a pot on a kitchen windowsill.

In the ground Choose a suitable spot and sow direct. Aim to establish a self-seeding patch that will look after itself. If the seed fails to germinate in one spot, try another.

Harvesting Pick large outer leaves first, leaving smaller leaves to grow on.

Seed saving This is relatively easy, although chervil sets seed in its second year. Allow the seedpods to turn brown and dry fully on the plant, or uproot the plant and bring it indoors to dry out. It may self-seed to save you the bother. Use seed quickly, as viability declines after one year.

Pests and diseases Largely trouble-free.

leaves, flowers   5/5

Preserving You can freeze the whole plant but texture deteriorates. It's better to mix into a herb butter with lemon juice and chopped capers (see page 182).

Notes

Chervil is a hardy biennial in the Apiaceae family, also known as the umbels, which includes carrots, parsley and dill. It is grown mostly as an annual.

The plant does not enjoy hot, direct sun, which can cause it to run to seed prematurely.

Left to flower in its second year, chervil will grow up to half a metre tall and produce clusters of tiny, white edible flowers.

2 WAYS WITH CHERVIL

Chervil has a delicate flavour, so don't overwhelm it with others. I tend to use it sparingly, adding a subtle aniseed note to mild dishes. It also makes a pretty garnish. Always add at the end of cooking. Chervil combines especially well with modest amounts of basil, chives, tarragon and parsley, as well as creamy sauces, poached fish, scallops and eggs.

❧ Add chopped chervil to beaten eggs for an omelette. Or get fancy and chop with parsley, chives and tarragon for the classic French *fines herbes* mix.

❧ For a rich sauce for peas, carrots or scallops, sauté a diced shallot in butter, add a splash of white wine, reduce by half, add cream, reduce again until the sauce thickens, then mix in the chopped chervil. Season to taste, adding a tiny pinch of sugar if too tart.

CHERVIL & TOMATO DRESSING

Serves 2

200g tomatoes
4 tablespoons olive oil
1 garlic clove, very finely chopped
1 teaspoon red wine vinegar
4 tablespoons chervil leaves, stalks
  removed

This is a classy, warm dressing for white fish. Diced tomatoes are lightly cooked in olive oil, flavoured with chervil, garlic and vinegar, then spooned over the fish. I can seldom be bothered to skin a tomato, but this recipe is a definite exception. Cook whatever white fish is best on the fishmonger's slab – plaice, sea bass, turbot or even scallops work well.

First, remove the skin from the tomatoes. With a sharp knife, score the skin with a cross at the bottom of the fruit, place in a bowl and cover with boiling water. Scoop out 10–20 seconds later, depending on size, drop into cold water, peel off the skin, slice and deseed. Dice the tomato flesh into 5–8mm squares.

Warm the oil in a small frying pan, then add the garlic and cook gently over a low heat for 3 minutes. Do not allow it to brown. Add the tomatoes and cook until warmed through. Add the red wine vinegar, stir, add the chervil and spoon over the fish.

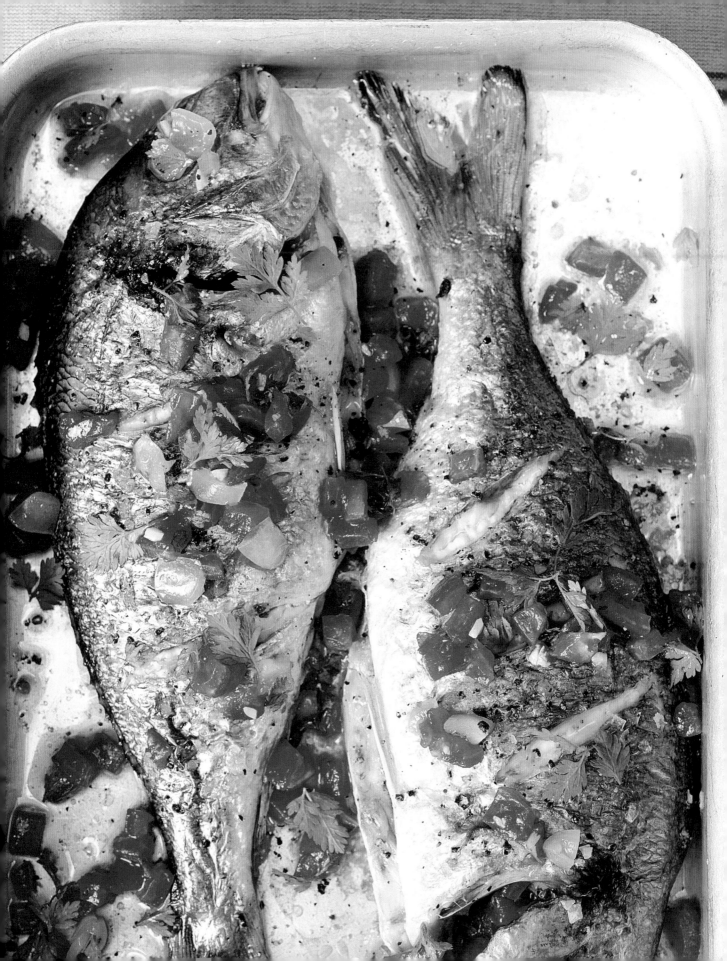

Coriandrum sativum
CORIANDER

It's the world's most popular herb, with a reputation for being tricky to grow. But do not fear – a few simple but cunning tactics will help to tame this temperamental plant.

To grow it well, treat coriander as a special case, unlike other herbs. It has a tendency swiftly to begin flowering and run to seed, especially in hot weather. This means you may have a window of just a few weeks, especially in the hotter months, to harvest the leaf. For this reason, sow a batch every two or three weeks for a steady supply, and grow in bulk. This way you can harvest coriander at different stages of the plant's life cycle, for example by cutting young leaves from one batch while saving seed from another.

Interestingly, coriander bucked the usual historical trends to spread from west to east. Native to Eastern Europe, it has now become a star ingredient in much of the Middle East, Mexico and Asia. My Bangladeshi neighbours grow it in abundance.

Coriander leaves are the main harvest but the spicy, young, green seeds are also sensational. And in my kitchen roasted dry coriander seeds are as ubiquitous as black pepper. The flowers, stems and roots also have distinctive flavours.

Recommended varieties Always use fresh seed no more than two years old. Coriander seed is large and sown prolifically, so consider buying in bulk or save your own seed. There is not a wide choice of varieties. Modern varieties such as 'Cilantro' are marketed as slower to run to seed, but pack sizes are often small. 'Confetti' is a modern variety worth growing for its feathery, tendril-like leaves.

It's possible to use the far cheaper large packs of culinary coriander seed from food shops. Choose the unpolished type, which is brown in colour. You will save cash but don't be surprised by lower germination rates and plants that run to seed swiftly. Note that Vietnamese coriander, a perennial, is not from the same plant family.

Growing Coriander prefers a spot in sun or light shade. The seed has a thick coat so soaking it overnight in warm water will hasten germination, though it is not essential. Sow from early spring to late summer, but note that the plant will be less happy in hotter months. It also dislikes being

leaves, seeds, flowers | 5/5

moved about. Sow directly where you want the herb to grow, either in straight drills or a patch. You could also sow coriander in plug trays, one seed per cell, and plant out as seedlings. Keep moist and well watered. *Spacing:* 3–8cm, depending on the size of plant you want to grow. Allow 15cm between rows.

Containers *Minimum compost depth:* 8cm. Ideally use a soil-based compost mix to preserve moisture. Choose wide, shallow containers to maximise surface area. I use recycled plastic vegetable trays (see page 171). I aim to have three trays on the go simultaneously – one recently sown; the other in leaf; the oldest running to seed. *Indoors:* You can grow coriander leaves indoors, but probably only in small volumes. If possible, grow in bulk outdoors.

In the ground Water the soil first and sow seed directly. Take care that the soil does not dry out. This is especially critical during germination.

Harvesting Coriander does not respond well to the cut-and-come-again treatment, so harvest the whole plant. Keeping the roots intact will prolong its storage life in the fridge.

Seed saving This is easy, ideally from a spring sowing. Leave a few plants to flower, choosing those that flower last. Wait until seed has turned brown. Harvest when dry and use the following year, as viability declines swiftly.

Pests and diseases Slugs may target seedlings. Otherwise, largely trouble-free.

Preserving Don't bother. The leaves can be frozen, but the texture deteriorates.

Notes

Coriander is a hardy annual in the Apiaceae family, also known as the umbels, which includes carrots, chervil, dill and parsley.

The leaf shape changes when the plant begins to flower. The flowers are edible and also attract beneficial insects such as hoverflies.

Set up a system to remind you to sow the seed regularly, for example with a fortnightly reminder on your mobile phone.

Green coriander seeds

6 WAYS WITH CORIANDER

Think of the different plant parts as having distinct uses. The stem becomes more pungent towards the root and the fresh green seeds are more intense than the dried seeds. The flowers have a delicate flavour. Coriander combines especially well with mint, parsley, chilli, garlic, citrus, cumin, tequila and avocado.

Above: 'Confetti' coriander

❀ Use the leaves in ceviche, the nifty South American technique where citrus juice 'cooks' the fish. Here's the basic technique: cut spanking fresh fish or scallops into slivers or cubes; sprinkle generously with fine salt and any spices; toss with chopped coriander and finely sliced onion and chilli; squeeze over copious citrus juice to cover the fish – lemon, lime, grapefruit, orange or a mixture; marinate from 5 minutes to overnight, depending on the size of fish and the degree of 'cooking' you prefer. Play around with extra flavours and textures, such as fresh or dried coriander seeds, fresh or pickled ginger, pepper, cumin, wasabi, sesame oil and crushed kaffir lime leaves.

❀ Rustle up a quick guacamole. In a bowl, mash the flesh from a ripe avocado with a fork. Add sea salt and lime juice to taste, then stir in chopped coriander leaves. Optional extras include tomato, onion and chilli.

❀ Whizz up the leaf in a coriander pesto (see page 92), in place of basil.

❀ Use the stalk and lower stem to make a Thai green curry paste.

❀ Mix the fresh green seed into fruit salads or yoghurt dips.

❀ Gently roast dried coriander seed in a heavy-bottomed pan until light brown and fragrant. Crush into crunchy fragments and experiment with sprinkling, like pepper, over savoury dishes. In fact, the two spices combine beautifully together.

FRESH CORIANDER & COCONUT CHUTNEY

This is a dip with zip and is highly addictive – I often eat it on its own with a teaspoon. South India is its spiritual home. This version uses desiccated coconut and coconut cream, which are widely available, but it's even better made with fresh coconut. I crack mine open with a hammer, prising out the flesh and shredding it in a food processor. Try this chutney in sandwiches, as a marinade for prawns, with rice or spread on fish fillets to bake in foil.

In a heavy-based frying pan, dry-roast the peanuts without oil until they start to colour, then tip into a bowl to cool. In a food processor, roughly blitz the cooled peanuts, chilli, garlic and cumin. Add the coconut and remaining ingredients, except the coriander and lime juice, topping up with 1 tablespoon water. Process to a paste. (You may need to nudge in any mixture that sticks to the sides of the processor, using a wooden spoon or spatula.) Add the coriander and blitz. Adjust the seasoning, mixing in the lime juice to taste. Aim for a balance of heat, sweetness and sourness.

Makes 1 small bowl (approx. 250g)

2 tablespoons skinless peanuts
1 fresh mild green chilli (or to taste)
½ garlic clove
Pinch of cumin
50g desiccated coconut
50g coconut cream
1½ teaspoons tamarind paste (optional)
1 teaspoon brown sugar
¼ teaspoon salt
100g coriander leaves and stalks, chopped
Juice of 2 limes (or to taste)

If using fresh coconut, substitute 100g of the flesh for the desiccated coconut and coconut cream.

CHOCOLATE TRUFFLES

Makes about 20 truffles

For the ganache:
125g dark chocolate
125g double cream
50g light muscovado sugar

For the truffle coating:
Cocoa powder

To customise – ideas for filling:
Green coriander seeds
Stem ginger, finely chopped
Cranberries, chopped

To customise – ideas for rolling:
Desiccated coconut
Crushed mixed nuts
Ground coffee beans
Sesame seeds

Truffles are considered the height of chocolate sophistication, but are actually a doddle to make. Just prepare the base and then customise as you like. While idly grazing on my roof garden, I recently discovered my new favourite flavouring – green coriander seeds. Picked when young and crunchy, the fresh green seeds have a fruity and spicy flavour that works brilliantly with dark chocolate.

In this recipe, the coriander seeds star as one of several flavourings but are not essential. You can happily make brilliant truffles without them. The recipe for the ganache is from my friend and chocolatier Paul A. Young. The truffles here are dusted with cocoa powder. The fancier option is to temper them with a thin layer of crisp chocolate, but this is a little more complicated. If tempted, you will find instructions in Paul's ace book Adventures with Chocolate.

First, break the chocolate into small, even-sized pieces and place in a medium-sized mixing bowl. Place the cream and sugar in a small saucepan. Bring to the boil and simmer for 1 minute. This will fully dissolve the sugar and kill any bacteria that may be present in the cream.

Turn off the heat and allow the cream to cool for 1 minute … Now pour your rested cream onto the chocolate pieces and mix well with a spatula until smooth and very glossy.

Allow the ganache to cool to room temperature, then place it, covered, in the fridge for at least 2 hours or until fully set.

To make the truffles, remove the ganache from the fridge. Use a teaspoon to scoop out even-sized pieces of the chocolate and place them onto a sheet of parchment paper. If you are filling the truffles, press the ingredients into the chocolate. (I add about 6 green coriander seeds per truffle.) Then dust your hands with cocoa powder and use your fingers to roll the ganache into even-sized spheres. To finish, dust the truffles in more cocoa or roll in other ingredients, such as desiccated coconut, if you fancy. Store the truffles in the fridge but eat at room temperature.

Mentha spicata, M. x piperita

MINT

Save your favourite large pots for your mint collection. There's a bewildering array of varieties and flavours, so choose carefully – not all are useful when cooking.

Much as I love the stuff, mint is definitely a two-faced herb: in the kitchen, it's charmingly fragrant; on the plot it's a thug, growing rampant if allowed free rein. So keep it restricted in pots and grow in bulk. I get through fistfuls of the stuff in cocktails and pots of mint tea, let alone when cooking.

Recommended varieties Nurseries sell a wide range, but don't get too carried away. Common garden mint is the mainstay. It is an example of a spearmint type which have a less intense flavour than peppermints. 'Chocolate Mint' is a peppermint, with a sophisticated flavour and well worth growing. 'Moroccan Mint' is essential if you like mint tea. 'Bowles's Mint' is excellent too. It's also handy to have a citrus-flavoured mint, such as 'Grapefruit Mint', for summer drinks and fruit salads.

Growing Mint is not over fussy and will grow in most soils. It prefers moist conditions and tolerates some shade. You can grow a few varieties of mint from seed, but don't bother. Instead, buy plants from herb nurseries or take a cutting from a friend's plant (see opposite). A single plant, once established, will keep going for years. *Spacing:* About 30cm between plants.

Containers *Minimum compost depth:* 15cm. Use a soil-based compost. Refresh the compost every spring: carefully tip the plant out of its container, scrape off any loose compost, then move into a slightly larger pot, planting with fresh compost. Use a general-purpose liquid feed. *Indoors:* You can grow mint indoors, but probably only in small volumes. If possible grow in bulk outdoors.

In the ground Bear in mind that mint spreads swiftly by sending out side roots, so is hard to control. One option is to plant the herb in a pot and then bury this in the ground to keep the mint in check, leaving the rim of the pot a few centimetres above soil level. Another option is to dig in a wall of tiles or a similar barrier around the plant's roots.

leaves, flowers | 5/5

Harvesting Regularly pinch out the growing tips to use in the kitchen. This will also help to maintain the plant's shape and balance (see page 17, but note that mint does not get especially bushy). The flowers are edible but strongly flavoured.

Propagation Either take stem cuttings in spring or summer (see page 178) or try root cuttings in winter: tip the plant out of its pot and snip off one or more lengths of root. Cut the root into sections 4–6cm long. Almost fill a pot with multipurpose compost mixed with extra grit for drainage, and then lay the root cuttings on top, allowing space between each one. Cover with a layer of compost, then water and leave to take root, checking every week.

You can also divide established plants in spring or autumn: use a spade or trowel to dig through a clump of mint and lift part of it with its roots; replant the lifted clump elsewhere and leave the original plant to grow on.

Pests and diseases Largely trouble-free.

Preserving Freeze small leaves and flowers in ice cubes (see page 182) then pop directly into drinks.

Notes

Mint is a hardy, herbaceous perennial in the large Lamiaceae family, also known as the labiates, which includes basil, rosemary, shiso, thyme and many others.

It is a useful plant for attracting beneficial insects such as butterflies and hoverflies.

From left: 'Chocolate Mint' and common garden mint

7 WAYS WITH MINT

Use young leaves raw and tougher leaves for sauces and general cooking. Mint flowers are edible but strongly flavoured. Mint combines especially well with chocolate, peas, new potatoes, mango, lemon, strawberries and other herbs, including basil, coriander, dill and lemon verbena.

✿ Infuse the flavours into melted chocolate to make a special cake icing or base for truffles (see page 68).

✿ To make Moroccan mint tea, which aids digestion after a meal, stew the leaves of Moroccan mint or other spearmint with green tea and sugar to taste. Chocolate mint also makes a lovely herbal tea, especially paired with sage leaves. Or try a duet of peppermint and lemon verbena.

✿ Use the leaves in classic cocktails such as a mojito or julep, or try chocolate mint in a Bourbon Stinger (see opposite).

✿ Make a tsatsiki, the Greek yoghurt-based dip: grate or thinly slice cucumber, sprinkle with salt, leave for half an hour in a colander, then squeeze to remove excess water. Mix with strained yoghurt, mint leaves, a little crushed garlic and salt. Serve chilled, with a swirl of olive oil and sprinkle of paprika.

✿ Apparently, there was an ancient Greek ritual of rubbing the dinner table with mint leaves before sitting down to eat – try it, to provoke a ravenous appetite.

✿ For special cheesy peas, add sprigs of mint to the cooking water when boiling frozen peas. Drain the peas, then mix with crumbled feta cheese and extra mint leaves.

✿ Combine mint with parsley in the classic Lebanese dish tabbouleh, made with bulghur wheat and tomatoes.

BOURBON STINGER COCKTAIL

In Hungary, a kocsma *is a traditional, low-key drinking den – my kind of place. My favourite is in a Budapest suburb, surrounded by large gardens where the locals grow tons of fruit and veg.*

It's also home to my friend Dez O'Connell, a cocktail guru, who invented this splendid drink. The inspiration was a patch of chocolate mint in his in-laws' garden – the herb pairs beautifully with bourbon whiskey.

This recipe looks complicated, but do not fear. Just infuse a bottle of bourbon the day before – any left over will keep indefinitely. The cocktail itself takes minutes to make. Serve in a whisky tumbler. You cannot scale this recipe up – make them with love, one at a time.

To infuse the spirit, place the mint leaves and bourbon in a large, clean, sealable jar. Shake gently and leave for 24 hours. The next day, shake again, then use a fine sieve to strain into a bottle of your choice. Taste the infusion. If the mint flavour is overpowering, add another 100ml or so of the remaining bourbon to mellow.

To make the cocktail, use a muddler or small rolling pin to press the orange zest firmly into the bottom of the glass, using a twisting motion. Add the sugar syrup and a dash of Angostura bitters.

Next, add 50ml of the infused bourbon and the ice – it's vital you do this in stages for a proper drink. Add 2 ice cubes and 20ml of the bourbon and stir gently with a long spoon until the ice just begins melt and dilute the spirit. Repeat with a further 20ml of the bourbon and 2 more ice cubes. Finally, add the remaining bourbon and ice cubes, stir again and serve.

Serves 1

2 x 6cm strips of orange zest, with as
   little pith as possible
1 teaspoon (5ml) sugar syrup (see
   page 69)
Dash of Angostura bitters
6 ice cubes

For the infused bourbon:
30 leaves of chocolate mint (approx.)
500ml bourbon whiskey (Jim Beam Black
   or Heaven Hill, for example)

Above: Chocolate Mint

VIETNAMESE SUMMER ROLLS

Serves 2, as a starter

For the dipping sauce:
4 tablespoons water
1 tablespoon granulated sugar
1 teaspoon rice wine vinegar
Juice of 1 lime
1–2 red chillies, deseeded and finely
  chopped
1 garlic clove, finely chopped
1 teaspoon finely grated fresh ginger
2 tablespoons fish sauce

For the rolls:
25g fine rice vermicelli
6 rice paper discs or wrappers (available
  in oriental stores)
200g cooked prawns, halved lengthways
  if large
Large handful of mixed herb leaves,
  such as mint, coriander, basil and
  green shiso, torn if large
6 lettuce or mustard leaves
30g bean sprouts

I love making these, and children enjoy rolling them too. It's a perfect grow-your-own recipe — there's no fixed list of ingredients, just add what's best from your plot. One essential is plenty of fresh mixed herbs, especially mint. Over the years, I've filled the rolls with all sorts, including mangetouts, pea shoots, shungiku, sorrel, garlic chives and radish leaves. For protein, prawns are used here, but you could substitute tofu, pork, beef or chicken.

Serve with the dipping sauce; light soy sauce works well too.

First, make the dipping sauce. In a small saucepan, heat the water, sugar and vinegar until the sugar has dissolved. Turn off the heat and allow to cool. Add the lime juice, chillies, garlic, ginger and fish sauce, stirring and tasting as you go to balance the flavours.

Cook the rice vermicelli, as per the packet's instructions. Refresh under cold water, drain and chop into lengths of roughly 8–10cm.

Get ready to roll — arrange each ingredient as on an assembly line: start with a large bowl of warm water to soak the rice paper discs or wrappers; next, you will need a plate, covered with a clean tea towel, on which to drape them once soaked; then the prawns, herb leaves, vermicelli and the other fresh ingredients, each in a separate bowl.

Soak a rice paper disc in the warm water for 15 seconds or until pliable. Transfer to the plate. Start to make a pile of the ingredients in the bottom third of the rice paper, arranging prawns and other ingredients to taste.

Roll up tightly from the bottom, fold in the sides, then finish rolling up the cylinder. The rice paper should be slightly sticky, which will help to seal the rolls.

Repeat the process for all the other rice paper discs, topping up the warm water with the kettle if necessary.

Slice the rolls on the diagonal and serve with the dipping sauce.

Ocimum basilicum. O.sanctum

BASIL

Rub the leaves – that fragrance, smudged onto your fingers, is what makes basils so special. Their foliage offers us fragile aromatic oils, which intensify with the heat of the sun.

Shops seldom offer much choice of basil varieties. They do, however, often sell the herb in pots, and you can pot up these seedlings as a sneaky short cut. Seed catalogues provide a wider range of varieties, promising distinct and exotic flavours such as cinnamon or lime. Resist the temptation to buy them all. Many basil varieties don't deliver in the kitchen, so grow only those that taste best.

Recommended varieties There are more than a hundred varieties of basil. Grow sweet basil, such as 'Genovese', in bulk. The smaller-leaved Greek basil is handy for salads, as you can add the leaves whole. 'Mrs Burn's Lemon Basil' has a refreshing hint of citrus. 'Thai' basil is more spicy and is used in Asian cooking. If you like to cook Thai food, also try the fragrant 'Holy' basil. Purple basils have irresistible colour, but be aware that the flavour is slightly less refined. The unusual perennial 'African Blue' is highly decorative, although less useful in the kitchen.

Growing Basil seed needs warmth to germinate, around 20°c minimum, and will sulk in wet weather and cold temperatures. So be patient, and sow when conditions are right.

Sow seed from late spring in a warm spot indoors, or outdoors in early summer when the weather has warmed up. Sow in plug trays, two seeds per cell, removing the weakest once germinated. Alternatively, sow direct where the plant will grow.

Basils crave sun, so position your plants accordingly. Pinch out the growing tip to make it more compact and bushy (see page 17). *Spacing:* 15–20cm between plants.

Containers *Minimum compost depth:* 10cm. Basil is best in pots. Plant seedlings in a multipurpose compost. Ideally, mix with grit or horticultural sharp sand to improve drainage. Use a general-purpose liquid feed. Try planting a mix of basil varieties in one pot, or plant with tomatoes for a classic combination. *Indoors:* Grow on a sunny windowsill. Bring in outdoor-grown plants if the weather deteriorates or at the end of the growing season.

leaves, flowers | 5/5

In the ground Basil is very happy in containers, so consider saving space in your soil for other crops.

Harvesting Try to harvest basil by pinching off the growing tip. This keeps the plant's growth in check and provides the best-tasting leaves. Cut or pinch off flowering spikes to prolong leaf production. For the most intense flavour, pick before watering and when the weather is dry and sunny.

Seed saving This is relatively straightforward if the plants are sown early enough in the season to bear seed. Varieties will cross, so choose one variety to save and let it flower while picking off the emerging flower stalks of any others. Alternatively, cover a flowering spike with fine mesh or similar. Wait until the seedpods dry thoroughly on the plant. Stored seed will last around 5 years.

Pests and diseases Aphids may target plants. Whitefly can be an issue with indoor-grown basil (see page 165).

Preserving Store fresh basil out of the fridge, away from direct sunlight. Pesto, of course, is the classic preserving recipe (see overleaf). You can also whizz or steep the leaves in olive oil, then store in the fridge or freezer for up to 3 months.

Notes

Basils are tender, half-hardy annuals in the Lamiaceae family, also known as the labiates, which includes mint, thyme, sage and rosemary. (There are a few exceptions that are perennial, such as 'African Blue'.)

Water little and often, taking care not to overwater. Ideally water in the morning or at lunchtime so the plants are not damp at night. Aim to soak the roots, not the leaves.

To save time, buy a pot of basil from a supermarket, separate the individual seedlings from the clump, and then repot the strongest in separate pots (see photo above). This will, however, limit your choice of varieties.

By autumn, outdoor plants may start to resent the cold weather. Basil is also very vulnerable to frost. Watch out for dark patches on the leaves, plucking off any that are damaged. Move plants indoors or harvest the whole plant.

6 WAYS WITH BASIL

These tender leaves appreciate delicate treatment. For most dishes, tear rather than chop the leaves, and add towards the end of cooking. The flowers are also edible. Basil pairs especially well with parsley, rosemary, thyme, tomatoes, courgettes, peas, strawberries, coconut, chicken and citrus.

❁ Infuse the fragrant leaves in a honey and basil daiquiri (see page 159).

❁ For a classy canapé, wrap a basil leaf around slow-roasted cherry or plum tomatoes (see page 58) or bocconcini, the bite-sized Italian soft cheeses. You can also add leaves to salads, sandwiches, mayonnaise, omelettes and aioli (see page 155).

❁ For a delicious pesto, work fast and with a light touch. Use plenty of basil, choosing the most pungent small leaves. Here's the process: toast pine nuts in the oven or dry-roast in a frying pan, then allow to cool. In a pestle and mortar, crush a little garlic (optional) with a pinch of sea salt; add torn basil leaves bit by bit, mashing gently, then the toasted pine nuts, and grated Parmesan and/or pecorino cheese. Slowly incorporate light virgin olive oil. You could also use a food processor, following the same order. Store in the fridge, topped with a layer of oil to seal. If you want to play around, try using walnuts, parsley and wild or new garlic.

❁ For a herbal tea, steep the leaves in hot water with a slice of fresh ginger and a teaspoon of honey.

❁ For a fruit surprise, try basil with strawberries, perhaps with a few drops of balsamic vinegar – a match, apparently, devised by food writer Anna del Conte, who also perfected a recipe for strawberry and balsamic ice cream.

❁ Infuse the flavour of basil leaves into a chocolate ganache to use for icing cakes or making truffles (see page 68).

THAI BASIL & CLAMS

When I last visited Bangkok, I checked out the local Tesco supermarket. They sold a special monk's bucket, which included candles, incense, washing-up liquid and shrimp-flavoured noodles. The thought of such abstinence made me ravenously hungry – here is my take on the street food that I ate to quell the pangs. Use plenty of 'Thai' basil, to show off its distinctive flavour. Serve with rice.

Rinse the clams thoroughly, swirling vigorously in a large bowl of cold water. If any are gaping open, tap them on the side of the sink. Discard if they do not slowly start to close.

Place a wok over the highest heat. Add the oil, then the garlic and ginger. Stir for 10 seconds, or until starting to colour, then add the chilli sauce, fish sauce and water, and stir to mix. Add the clams and stir again. Place a lid or plate over the wok to trap the steam and cook for 2–4 minutes, or until all the clams are open and piping hot. Stir through the basil, cover, and steam for a further 10 seconds, then serve.

Serves 2, as a main course

500g live clams
1 tablespoon peanut oil or vegetable oil
2 garlic cloves, finely chopped
1 tablespoon finely chopped fresh
  ginger
1 tablespoon sweet chilli dipping sauce
1 teaspoon fish sauce
4 tablespoons water
Handful of 'Thai' basil leaves (approx.
  10g), chopped

If you struggle to find clams, this recipe also works well with mussels.

Purple basil, sweet basil and lemon basil

BASIL & LIME ICE CREAM

Serves 6

25g sweet basil leaves
150g caster sugar
200g mascarpone or double cream
400ml full-fat yoghurt
Zest of ½ a lime

A knock-out idea, best made with sweet basil. I first heard of it when visiting Sarah Raven, the gardening and cookery writer, in the rolling Sussex hills — a far cry from my urban patch. She, in turn, had first tasted it in De Kas restaurant in Amsterdam, where they grow much of their own produce. I have adapted the original recipe to include the zest of half a lime, which further lifts the incredible flavour. You can use double cream or mascarpone, which lends a superior texture. Eat within a week.

Blitz the basil and sugar in a food processor or blender. Add the other ingredients and blitz again, until no lumps remain. Either pour into an ice-cream maker and churn for 20 minutes, then transfer to a plastic container and freeze. Or, if you don't have an ice-cream maker, pour straight into a plastic container, freeze for 2 hours, then slide a fork around the edges to mix and break up the ice crystals, as you are aiming for a smooth texture. Repeat this process every hour until the ice cream is solid.

Perilla frutescens

SHISO

This brilliant plant is seldom grown for eating in the West, yet in Japan it's an everyday herb, like basil in Italy, or coriander in Mexico. Pepsi even brewed a special cola with shiso flavour.

In my kitchen, shiso has been a recent discovery and total revelation. I experiment with the green leaves where I might use basil or mint, and try my hand at classic Japanese dishes. The jagged leaves grow large and are also excellent as a wrap or for decorating a plate.

There are two main types of shiso, green and purple. Pay more attention to green shiso, which has a bright, uplifting and floral aroma. Purple shiso is more of a decorative plant and traditionally used to colour pickles such as Japanese umeboshi apricots.

Shiso is also popular in several other Asian countries, including Korea and Vietnam. The flowers and seeds are edible too.

Recommended varieties Green and purple shiso occupy either end of the spectrum, with some varieties sharing traits of both. The best flavour is found in Japanese green shiso, which typically has crinkly leaves and an invigorating, almost minty aroma. I grow this in bulk. Korean varieties have larger leaves, often tinged with purple on the underside, but possess a less refined flavour. Purple shiso is worth growing only if you have space. It has a fruity, spicy scent with a hint of cloves and cinnamon.

Growing Shiso prefers a sheltered spot in sun. Sow at a similar time to basil: indoors in mid-spring, for potting up and planting later, or sow directly into its final position in early summer. I sow into plug trays, two seeds per cell, later removing the weaker plant. *Spacing:* About 25cm between plants.

Containers *Minimum compost depth:* 15cm. Ideally use a soil-based compost, sowing seed direct into the compost or planting established seedlings. Try growing green and purple shiso together in a container for a colourful display. Use a general-purpose liquid feed. *Indoors:* Shiso does well indoors. Treat in the same way as basil (see page 90).

In the ground Shiso prefers a well-drained soil, and can grow into a large plant.

leaves, seeds, flowers · 5/5

Harvesting Pick younger leaves for the finest flavour. Large leaves can grow to a significant size.

Seed saving This is relatively easy. Bear in mind that the various coloured varieties will cross, so grow only one type if you want to save seed. Collect seed from the dried seedpods after flowering. The plants can also be left to self-seed.

Pests and diseases Largely trouble-free.

Preserving Preserve the leaves in a herb butter (see page 182). The leaves of purple shiso can be used to colour pickles.

Notes

Shiso is a bushy, half-hardy annual in the Lamiaceae family, also known as the labiates, which includes basil, mint, rosemary, thyme and many others. It is also known as perilla and the beefsteak plant.

Shiso is often also used as an ornamental plant in flower beds, which is proof of its visual appeal.

Once established, pinch out the growing tip to encourage a bushy plant (see page 17).

Clockwise from top left: purple shiso, Japanese green shiso and Korean shiso

8 WAYS WITH SHISO

Green shiso is most useful in the kitchen. Eat the young leaves raw or add at the end of cooking. Large shiso leaves can withstand rougher treatment: shred or use whole leaves to decorate a plate, arranging food on top. Green shiso pairs especially well with coriander, ginger, horseradish, tomatoes, strawberries and Japanese ingredients such as miso (fermented soy bean paste), seaweed and umeboshi (Japanese apricots pickled with purple shiso).

❀ Substitute green shiso for basil and mint in your favourite recipes. For example, toss torn leaves into Mediterranean-style tomato salads. Or try in a strawberry fruit salad, replacing basil (see page 128).

❀ Make your own sashimi, the classic Japanese dish of sliced raw fish. Buy thick, skinless fillets of extremely fresh mackerel, sea bream, sea bass or good-quality farmed salmon. Slice and serve with green shiso leaves, pickled ginger and bowls of wasabi and soy sauce.

❀ Substitute green shiso for dill when home-curing mackerel (see page 73).

❀ Include green or purple shiso leaves in a tempura assortment (see page 119), or wrap into Vietnamese summer rolls (see page 88).

❀ Get creative with shiso cocktails. Infuse vodka with green shiso, then shake up a terrific ice-cold martini with a splash of vermouth. Or try shiso as a replacement for mint in mojitos.

❀ Try the simple Japanese dish of *hiyayakko*. Cut chilled silken tofu into portion-sized squares, then decorate the top with finely chopped green shiso, finely grated fresh ginger, slices of spring onion and a dash of soy sauce.

❀ Stir shredded green shiso leaves into fried rice dishes. Or add to maki rolls (sushi rice wrapped in a sheet of seaweed), perhaps with a nugget of pickled ume, the Japanese apricot.

❀ Infuse the flavour of green or purple shiso leaves into a chocolate ganache to use for icing cakes or making truffles (see page 68).

SHISO GRANITA

Wonderfully refreshing, this delicious dessert is best served up as a surprise — friends can guess the mystery flavour. Granita is an ice from Sicily, similar to a sorbet, but with more chunky, melt-in-the-mouth crystals. Place a small, shallow, metal baking tray in the freezer before you start to make it.

This is a simple recipe, but you will need to stick around for the first few hours of freezing to stir and break up the crystals every hour or so. Serve instantly in a martini glass or fancy teacup with a teaspoon, with a small shiso leaf to decorate.

Serves 4

420ml water
80g caster sugar
45ml freshly squeezed lemon juice
30g green shiso leaves (approx. 20 medium-sized leaves), torn, plus 4 small leaves to garnish

Put all the ingredients (apart from the garnish) in a blender and whizz until the shiso is thoroughly chopped. Allow to stand for 5 minutes. Strain this liquid through a fine sieve into the chilled baking tray, then freeze.

Check 1½ hours later, running a fork around the edge of the tray to stir and break up the crystals. Repeat the process every 30 minutes, until you have crystals of uniform size. This will take around 3 hours in total.

Allow the granita to thaw slightly before serving, fluffing up the crystals with a fork. Garnish each portion with a small shiso leaf. To store in the freezer, transfer to a sealable plastic container and eat within a fortnight.

Rumex acetosa, R. scutatus

SORREL

The zippy, lemony taste of sorrel is unique among herbs. This refreshing acidity is brilliantly useful in the kitchen, especially for sauces and salads, yet shops rarely stock sorrel – frankly, I can't grow enough of the stuff.

The plant is a hardy perennial, so aim to establish a permanent patch to offer a year-round supply.

Recommended varieties There are several varieties of sorrel, including wild field types and the unrelated wood sorrel, which are both popular with foragers. The best for a domestic plot are common sorrel (*Rumex acetosa*), which is widely available, and the smaller buckler-leaved variety (*R. scutatus*), which is particularly good for salads; an especially lovely variegated form of this is 'Silver Shield'. You may come across red-veined sorrel (*R. sanguineus var. sanguineus*) often touted as a sexy alternative. It's a stunner, but – as is so often the way – it lacks much flavourful character.

Growing Sorrel enjoys moist soil and can tolerate a touch of shade. Sow the seed in spring. You can start the seed off in plug trays, about five seeds per cell, to plant out as a clump. Alternatively, sow seed directly where the plant is to grow. *Spacing:* 10-20cm apart for large plants.

Containers *Minimum compost depth:* 15cm. The smaller buckler-leaved sorrel is your best bet. Sorrel prefers slightly acidic conditions, so ideally use ericaceous (acidic) compost. Water regularly and never let the container dry out. Use a general-purpose liquid feed. *Indoors:* Most suitable when grown for smaller baby leaves.

In the ground Sorrel is low-maintenance, ideal for a semi-shady spot.

Harvesting Pick regularly, as the leaves will regrow. Harvest young for superior flavour and texture; larger leaves are best in sauces. If the plant starts to send up flowering spikes, snip them off to prolong leaf production.

Propagation If you have established plants that are outgrowing their spot, you can divide the clump in spring or autumn. Use a spade or trowel to dig through the clump and lift part of it with its roots; replant the lifted clump elsewhere and leave the original plant to grow on.

leaves · 4/5

Pests and diseases Largely trouble-free.

Preserving You can freeze the leaves, washed and dried, but their texture deteriorates. Sorrel pesto is a better option (see page 92).

Notes

Sorrel is a hardy herbaceous perennial in the Chenopodiaceae family, also known as goosefoots, which includes beetroot.

Sorrel should survive the winter. The leaves may well die back during colder months, but the plant will bounce back in spring. Try protecting with a layer of horticultural fleece to extend the season.

To maintain your sorrel patch, harvest regularly and sow fresh seed to fill any gaps.

If you have a garden, buckler-leaved sorrel can make useful ground cover in areas of moist shade.

Common sorrel

7 WAYS WITH SORREL

Use the acidity of sorrel to add zip to your food. (Lemon juice performs a similar role.) It also cuts against the richness of oily fish. With larger leaves, strip out the midribs. Add sorrel at the end of the cooking process to preserve the vibrancy of flavour. The green colour turns brown with heat, so you could add extra chopped fresh leaves just before serving to boost colour. Sorrel leaves contain tiny amounts of oxalic acid – a natural substance that is harmful in large quantities, so do not eat handfuls every day. The herb goes especially well with mint, mustards, rocket, eggs, potatoes and fish.

Buckler-leaved sorrel

* Add sorrel sparingly to salads, tearing up larger leaves. To balance, tone down the vinegar or lemon juice in any dressing. For a punchy green salad, mix torn sorrel leaves with handfuls of wild rocket.
* For a sorrel sauce for fish, chop or snip sorrel into ribbons and gently cook in a little butter. Add a splash of double cream, reduce to thicken, stir in a beaten egg yolk, season and serve.
* For a quick lunch, gently fry sliced onions, garlic and fresh ginger, then add a tin of rinsed cooked chickpeas and a tin of tomatoes. Simmer to thicken, then stir in chopped sorrel and a pinch of ground cumin and/or paprika. Serve with a dollop of yoghurt.
* Include sorrel leaves when cooking other leafy greens such as spinach, mustards or chard.
* Toss sorrel leaves into a bowl of buttered new potatoes or slip in a layer of leaves when assembling a slow-baked potato gratin.
* Make a sorrel soup, adding to a base of cooked onion, potatoes, stock and thyme. Liquidise and serve, adding crème fraîche for a luxurious touch.
* Show off sorrel leaves in an omelette or soufflé (see page 145).

SALMON & SORREL SAUCE

This is a French classic and stylish quick supper. It was the Troisgros brothers, a legendary French family of chefs, who first made this recipe famous. My version is simplified for the home cook. Serve with mash or rice and steamed vegetables.

Warm two plates in the oven. To start the sauce, melt the butter in a heavy-based pan and gently fry the shallot until soft. Add the white wine, turn up the heat and allow to bubble until the liquid is reduced by around half. Add the cream and reduce again until the sauce thickens. Turn off the heat and cover to keep warm. You will add the sorrel just before serving.

Season the salmon fillets with salt and pepper. Heat the oil in a heavy-based frying pan, then fry the fillets for about 3 minutes on either side over a medium-high heat. Cook the fish swiftly, aiming to brown and crisp up the two sides of the fillets while keeping the middle moist and pink. Transfer to the warm plates and return them to the oven while you finish the sauce.

Bring the sauce back to a bubble, add the sorrel, stir, then season to taste with salt, pepper and a few drops of lemon juice.

Serves 2, as a main course

2 salmon fillets (approx. 150g each)
Salt and freshly ground pepper
½ tablespoon olive oil

For the sauce:
10g butter
1 shallot, finely diced
150ml dry white wine
80ml double cream
Large handful of chopped sorrel leaves
Squeeze of lemon juice

Thymus vulgaris

THYME

Treat it mean – that's the secret. Thyme demands sun but little else. Like rosemary, the plant thrives best in an arid Mediterranean climate so too much love actually encourages sappy growth and feeble flavour.

Herb nurseries stock dozens of different types of thyme, but just a handful shine in the kitchen. Common thyme is tough and withstands robust cooking. I also grow lemon and orange thymes, which are softer and more delicate. Thyme flowers are an occasional, colourful treat.

Recommended varieties There are multiple species and cultivars of thyme, flowering from white to purple. Many are more ornamental than culinary. Common thyme is essential, and more robust than 'Lemon Thyme', whose milder leaves can be scattered raw in salads. 'Orange Thyme' and 'Caraway Thyme' are worth a try. Creeping, wilder types are handy for filling in the gaps between stonework in garden paths.

Growing Don't attempt to grow thyme from seed. It's possible for some varieties, but seldom worth the bother. Buy established plants from herb nurseries or take cuttings from friends. Choose a sunny position. *Spacing:* About 25cm between plants.

Containers *Minimum compost depth:* 15cm. Use a soil-based compost. Aim for a mix that is low in nutrients and well drained. Add up to one third of grit or horticultural sharp sand to the mix. This will also help to dilute nutrient levels in the compost. Keep watering to a minimum, especially during winter. The compost should be more dry than moist. *Indoors:* Thyme will do fine on a bright windowsill.

In the ground Thyme needs poor soil with good drainage, so add handfuls of grit or horticultural sharp sand to the planting hole if necessary.

Harvesting Snip off whole sprigs. If you want to then strip off the leaves, slide your thumb and forefinger along the stem. Harvest at any time, but remember that the flavour peaks just before flowering in summer.

Propagation Raise new plants from cuttings taken in spring or summer (see page 178).

leaves, flowers   5/5

Pests and diseases Thyme is largely trouble-free.

Preserving Unlike most other herbs, common thyme retains decent flavour when dried. You could also make a thyme oil (see basil oil on page 91).

Notes

Thyme is a woody evergreen perennial herb in the large Lamiaceae family, also known as the labiates, which includes basil, mint, rosemary, shiso and many more.

Bees love flowering thyme, so it is excellent for attracting pollinators to your plot.

Left to its own devices, thyme can grow straggly. To keep it in shape, use secateurs to give it a gentle haircut in spring once it starts to grow. Prune it more heavily after it flowers in summer, cutting back the most woody, fibrous stems by two thirds.

4 WAYS WITH THYME

Either add whole sprigs to dishes as they cook, plucking them out before serving, or finely chop the softer leaves, often from the top of the plant, to eat raw. Thyme complements tomatoes, onions, lamb, chicken and white meaty fish and combines well with rosemary.

❀ For a sofa snack, rustle up a bowl of thyme popcorn. Choose a large pan with a lid, add enough cooking oil just to coat the bottom, then turn the heat to high. Add 70g of popping corn and 1 tablespoon thyme leaves, stir well, cover and cook, shaking the pan constantly, until all the corn has popped. Serve with melted butter and sea salt. For a decadent touch, heat 30g each of honey, butter and brown sugar until bubbling, then pour over the popcorn.

❀ Experiment by subtly infusing the flavour of sprigs of thyme into sweet dishes such as poached fruits, custards and crumbles.

❀ Make some herby breadcrumbs to add crunch to dishes. Pulse stale bread in a food processor with thyme leaves, lemon zest, salt and pepper. Sprinkle over fish pies, vegetable bakes or gratins before cooking. You can also fry the breadcrumbs until crisp in olive oil, then sprinkle over soups or pasta. I prefer my breadcrumbs coarse, not fine. This technique also works well with other herbs.

❀ Make your own za'atar, the Middle-Eastern spice mix. Dry-roast sesame seeds in a heavy-based pan, then grind up with salt, a small pinch of cumin, thyme leaves and sumac, a Middle-Eastern spice made from ground wild berries. Sprinkle over homemade flatbreads or pizzas, or jazz up roasted potatoes.

ANCHOÏADE

This magical substance takes moments to make and fires up the taste buds. Serve it on crunchy toast or slices of baguette, or as a dip for baby veg. It's terrific with a glass of red wine before supper.

Anchoïade originated in southern France. Strictly speaking, it should not include thyme. But this twist is inspired by Flip Dunning, who quit her job in advertising to sell her special Pâté Moi mushroom pâté, invented by her brother at the age of eight. The method below assumes you don't have a food processor. If you do, then you can skip the chopping and add all the ingredients in one go.

Pound the anchovies, olives, tomato, garlic, olive oil and softened butter to a smooth paste in a pestle and mortar. Season to taste with the lemon juice, vinegar, cognac and black pepper. Stir in the parsley and thyme.

To serve on toast, grill the bread slices on one side only, flip and spread the paste, then return to the grill until bubbling.

Serves 4, as an appetiser

1 tin anchovy fillets (30g), drained of oil
4 black or green olives
1 medium-sized tomato or 4 cherry
  tomatoes
1 large garlic clove, crushed
1 tablespoon olive oil
1 tablespoon softened butter
Small squeeze of lemon juice
½ teaspoon red wine vinegar
Few drops of cognac (optional)
Freshly ground black pepper
2 tablespoons finely chopped parsley
  leaves
1 teaspoon finely chopped lemon thyme
  leaves
Sliced baguette, to serve

LEAVES FOR SALAD

112 **MUSTARDS**

116 **SHUNGIKU**

120 **LETTUCES**

A decent salad is the cornerstone of the urban plot. I think of salads as a celebration of home-grown leafy vegetables – a palette of colours, flavours, textures and leaf shapes that sparkle with freshness. It's a dish we can produce on a daily basis, ever-changing through the seasons, but always shaming the puffy yet paltry salad bags sold in supermarkets.

I grow more salad than anything else. I climb out onto my roof garden and snip leaves straight into my salad bowl – they are on the plate minutes later.

Salad leaves score on many fronts as a good urban crop: they are easy and swift to grow, yet pricey in shops; they lose nutrients quickly once picked; many are quite happy in a spot of shade; and if you choose the right varieties you can eat fresh salad right through winter.

I have included my favourite leaves in this book, both in this section and in others. Lettuce is clearly essential, mustards are a diverse and under-appreciated bunch, and shungiku has a wonderful and distinct flavour.

There are dozens of other leaves you could also grow. Rainbow chard is excellent – colourful, hardy and cut-and-come-again. Spicy landcress is much like watercress but far easier to grow. Winter purslane has a succulent and unique texture. Also explore chicory, corn salad, endive, Mexican tree spinach, mibuna, mizuna, orache, pak choi, summer purslane and rocket, among many others.

Balance Salads can range in ambition from a bowl of wild rocket leaves, dressed only with drops of lemon juice, to complex creations of a dozen ingredients glistening with a sophisticated dressing.

Balance is at the heart of them all. Each ingredient should be distinct, yet not outshine any other. Taste and experiment as you assemble. I gather a selection of leaves in my fingers to test. All offer their own taste, texture and colour. The flavour table below may help with your mix:

Peppery	Bitter	Neutral	Sweet	Tart
Nasturtium	Beetroot leaf	Lettuce	Carrot leaf	Sorrel
Mustard	Chard	Purslanes	Pea shoots	
Radish leaf	Chicory	Corn Salad		
Landcress	Endive	Mexican Tree Spinach		
Mizuna	Shungiku	Mibuna		
Rocket		Orache		
		Pak Choi		

Herbs Herbs add character – use generously and try combining them: pair dill with mint, for example, or basil with parsley. Add sorrel for zip, or snip in some chives for a mild onion flavour. Use your fingers to tear up larger, more pungent herb leaves.

Colour Go for contrast, either bold or subtle: perhaps dark red lettuces or mustards among emerald leaves, or a dozen shades of green leaves. Edible flowers provide peerless bursts of colour. Always add them at the last moment, after any salad dressing, to keep the petals dry.

Texture Play around with varied textures: Cos lettuce, for example, has more crunch than a loose-leaf variety; winter purslane has a firm juiciness. To keep leaves in peak condition, tear or cut at the last moment. I tend to use my fingers, but a sharp knife will also minimise damage to plant cells. To perk up tired leaves, soak in a bowl or sink of cold water for half an hour, then dry and serve. Extra ingredients, of course, add distinct texture: toasted or sprouted seeds, slices of radish, grated carrot, chunks of roasted beetroot – the possibilities are never-ending.

Drying leaves Leaves must be dry in the salad bowl – soppy salads are unacceptable. I try not to wash my leaves if I can help it, just checking they are clean and not harbouring insects. With shop-bought leaves, invest in a big salad spinner. Add a sheet of kitchen paper when you spin-dry leaves to absorb moisture. Alternatively, wash and then dry them with a clean tea towel.

The dressing Sometimes leaves are best enjoyed naked; an oily dressing can be their ruin. A sprinkle of sea salt and lemon juice may do the trick. Or serve up dressings in separate bowls, to dip leaves as you fancy.

At heart, every good salad dressing is a balance of acid (vinegar or citrus juice), oil and salt. Aim for an intense, salty dressing – a blast of flavour. Ideally make them at least half an hour before using to allow the flavours to mingle. For sweetness, try honey or brown sugar.

Experiment with different vinegars and oils: sherry or raspberry vinegar, for example, can liven up bland flavours; walnut oil is fragrant and has a distinctive taste; grapeseed oil is more neutral; olive oils vary in fruitiness. Have a go with with hemp seed, rapeseed, cobnut, avocado and other less familiar oils. Strongly flavoured oils can be diluted with milder ones such as sunflower or groundnut. If a dressing seems too thick, loosen with a tablespoon or two of water.

Brassica juncea

MUSTARDS

I love foods with a fiery kick, so mustards are a must on my plot. They are quick and extremely easy to grow, and are invaluable as a winter crop.

I sow a batch every month or so, tossing a mix of seeds from different packets into my rooftop containers (see page 171). The leaves are ready in a few weeks, will cut-and-come-again three or more times, and can be snipped straight into the salad bowl.

Mustards are, however, a confusing family of plants, often grouped with 'orientals' in seed catalogues. There are hundreds of varieties in vibrant colours, from emerald greens to moody purples. Some are wonderful, others disappointing, so choose carefully. The worst mustards are little more than weeds repackaged as the desirable exotic. (In case you are wondering, mustard – the familiar pungent paste – is made from large quantities of ground mustard seed.)

Recommended varieties Experiment and choose your favourites. Mine include 'Green in Snow', which has feather-shaped, serrated leaves that are hot and juicy, with a firm texture. 'Golden Streaks' offers mild heat and striking leaf shape. 'Dragon's Tongue' is mild, with lovely, purple-veined leaves. 'Amsoi' is also mild with a bright emerald-green colour. Other good choices include 'Vietnamese', 'Red Giant' and 'Ruby Streaks'.

Growing Mustards are cool-season crops and are not fussy about where they grow. Mustards germinate and grow easily, will tolerate a touch of shade and require little aftercare. Either sow in early spring or after mid-summer to last through winter. Late-summer sowings tend to be the most successful. Early sowings are best for baby leaves, as plants will quickly run to seed during the hottest months.

For baby salad leaves you can grow the plants in clumps. Sow seed in plug trays, about five seeds per cell, and plant out as seedlings. Or scatter the seed evenly over the growing area, watering first, then gently rub the seed into the moist soil or compost. Spare a thought for colour when sowing – the various greens and purples can be used for creative effect. *Spacing:* 8–20cm for larger plants.

Containers *Minimum compost depth:* 10cm. I grow most of my mustards in shallow crates (see page 171). You could plant clumps of mustard, sown

leaves, flowers · 5/5

first in plug trays, or sow seed direct. Mustards are not fussy about the compost mix. *Indoors:* Mustards are a handy indoor crop if grown for baby salad leaves.

In the ground Sow direct and thin out if cramped. Alternatively, plant out seedlings.

Harvesting The leaves are best if harvested when young. Mustards can be grown as a cut-and-come-again crop, so you can snip off the larger leaves three or more times, leaving the remainder of the plant to grow on.

Seed saving Not straightforward. Different varieties will cross, and you need multiple plants to maintain genetic strength.

Pests and diseases Largely trouble-free. Holes in the leaves indicate flea beetle: the leaves will still be edible, but grow plants under horticultural fleece if this is a concern.

Preserving Best eaten fresh, as there is no satisfactory method.

Notes

Mustards are annuals and biennials in the Brassicaceae (brassica) family, which includes radishes, rocket and kale. There are various species of mustard.

Like other leafy salads, mustards require regular watering and may run to seed when stressed.

Heat levels vary between varieties and even individual plants. In general, they get hotter as they increase in size. The plants will also increase their heat if they are allowed to dry out.

Large plants, especially the redder and purple varieties, are decorative in their own right.

6 WAYS WITH MUSTARDS

Make the most of their varied colours and leaf shapes. Taste them as you go, because mustards vary in intensity. Smaller leaves are best in salads – I often add a handful for their colour and spicy flavour. Larger leaves are more pungent, but this will dissipate if exposed to heat, for example when tossed in a wok or blanched in boiling water. Mustards combine especially well with dill, mint, milder salad leaves, garlic and ginger.

* Exploit their colour to decorate a plate. The small leaves of the redder mustard varieties are particularly striking. Chefs buy mustards by the punnet as tiny microgreens, with just one or two pairs of leaves. For your own microgreen harvest, sow seed very thickly in seed trays.
* In salads, balance mustards with the milder flavours of leaves such as lettuce or pea shoots. The flavour of mustards responds well to a lemony vinaigrette.
* Use the leaves in Vietnamese summer rolls (see page 88) or in place of lettuce for Korean wraps (see page 122).
* For a terrific steak sandwich, spread sourdough bread with English mustard, add the meat and stuff in a handful of mixed mustard leaves.
* Cook the larger leaves when you might use spinach or other leafy greens, mixing them together if you fancy. Try steaming a large handful of mustard leaves and dress with olive oil, a sprinkle of sea salt and a squeeze of lemon juice.
* Try mustard leaves in a curry in place of beetroot leaves (see page 24) or combine with spinach for an Indian saag paneer, made with cubes of paneer cheese.

Chrysanthemum coronarium

SHUNGIKU

We are creatures of habit, and this plant proves the point. According to the food and science writer Harold McGee, there are around 300,000 edible plants in existence but humans only cultivate a few thousand.

Shungiku is a member of the chrysanthemum family. In the West we know chrysanthemums as a garden flower, but this tasty type is popular as a vegetable and salad leaf in countries such as Japan and China.

The flavour of the leaves is remarkable – strong, slightly bitter and aromatic. Some of my friends dislike it; most ask for more. I add the young leaves to salads, almost like a herb. Larger leaves are best thought of as a vegetable, lovely in hotpots and soups. Shungiku ticks all the boxes and a few plants are all you need.

Note that the plant also appears in seed catalogues as chop suey greens, Japanese greens, and garland chrysanthemum. The stem and petals of the flowers are edible too.

Recommended varieties You won't find a wide choice in seed catalogues. Leaf shape may range from small and serrated to large and more rounded.

Growing Shungiku is easy to grow. Sow in spring or late summer to grow through winter. Avoid sowing in mid-summer. You can either sow in plug trays, one seed per cell, then plant out the seedlings, or sow direct where you want the crop to grow. *Spacing:* About 30cm between plants.

Containers *Minimum compost depth:* 20cm. Use any multipurpose compost. One bushy plant makes a fine centrepiece for a medium-sized container. Use a general-purpose liquid feed for large, established plants. *Indoors:* Easy to grow on a bright windowsill.

In the ground Shungiku will grow happily in most soils.

Harvesting Pungency increases with the age of the plant. Focus your appetite on the young leaves and tender stems. Only the petals of the flower are edible, so carefully pluck them from the central parts of the flower.

Propagation Raise new plants from cuttings taken in spring or summer (see page 178). These will be softer and shorter than semi-ripe cuttings,

leaves, flowers

5/5

but are prepared in the same way. You can also save the seed from the dried flower heads.

Pests and diseases Largely trouble-free.

Preserving Best eaten fresh, or try in a pesto (see page 92).

Notes
Shungiku is an annual in the Asteraceae (formerly Compositae) family, which includes other chrysanthemums, lettuce, chicory and endives.

The plant does not thrive in very hot weather and may run to seed.

Beneficial insects are attracted to the flowers.

Use the technique of pinching out the growing tips to create a bushy plant, as it can reach up to 50cm in height if left untended (see page 17).

5 WAYS WITH SHUNGIKU

Add tender young leaves to salads. Larger leaves are more strongly flavoured and are best cooked before eating. The petals of the flowers are also edible. Shungiku pairs especially well with chervil, dill, milder salad leaves and eggs.

* Serve ohitashi style – a simple Japanese technique for cooking vegetables. Blanch about 50g shungiku leaves in boiling water for 1 minute, drain, refresh in cold water, then squeeze to remove excess water. Chop and serve with a sprinkle of sesame seeds and a sweet sesame dressing: mix 1 tablespoon tahini, 1 teaspoon caster sugar and 1 tablespoon light soy sauce.
* Add shungiku leaves to a salad of baby carrots and radish (see page 42).
* Include the leaves in Vietnamese summer rolls (see page 88) and Korean-style wraps (see page 122).
* Just before serving, add the leaves to communal hotpot dishes or soups such as my 'Feel Better' Broth (see page 51).
* Chop and add the leaves to herb mixes for omelettes.

The intense flavour of shungiku works brilliantly in a mix for tempura

TEMPURA

Celebrate your plot with this Japanese technique for a light-as-air, crisp batter. There's no prescribed ingredients — just serve up your favourite bits of your plants. Shungiku leaves work particularly well because of their distinctive flavour.

I make tempura as a crunchy treat for a friend or two, frying in small batches, and chatting in between each round. It's definitely not a dinner-party dish.

Play around with ingredients, aiming for contrasts of texture, colour and flavour. King prawns are my favourite, along with courgette flowers and paper-thin slices of fresh ginger, lemon or orange. Strips of courgette, peas in their pod, nasturtium flowers, sage leaves and baby carrots are also very good.

Make the batter immediately before cooking. Unless you are nifty with chopsticks, use tongs or your fingers to drop the vegetables into the batter, shake off any excess, then drop into the oil and remove with a slotted spoon. Purists dip their tempura only into salt.

First, to make the soda water really icy cold for the batter, pour it into a bowl or jug and place in the freezer for 30 minutes. Or add a handful of ice cubes, stir, then tip out the ice.

To make the dipping sauce, mix the ingredients together and pour into a small bowl.

To make the batter, mix the flour and cornflour together in a bowl, then tip them into the bowl or jug containing the ice-cold soda water. Use a fork or chopsticks to mix the batter swiftly for 15 seconds — you want a thin, light batter with a few floury lumps.

Pour the sunflower and sesame oil into a deep, heavy-bottomed, stable saucepan; it should be no more than a third full. Turn on the heat.

While the oil heats, get organised: lay a sheet of kitchen paper on a plate for draining the tempura; put the extra tablespoon of plain flour in a bowl for dusting; then check if the oil is sufficiently hot. To test, drop in a teaspoon of batter — it should sink to the bottom, then rise quickly. The oil is not hot enough if it rises slowly; it's too hot if it barely sinks. (If you have a thermometer, aim for 180°C.)

To fry, pick up each item with your fingers, dust with plain flour, shake off any excess, dunk in the batter, shake off any excess again, then carefully drop into the oil. Repeat for the other items and fry in small batches, using a slotted spoon to scoop out the cooked tempura and also remove any leftover scraps of fried batter as you go. Drain the tempura on the kitchen paper and eat swiftly while hot and crisp. Serve with the dipping sauce and sea salt.

Serves 2

For the batter:
300ml ice-cold sparkling soda water
100g plain flour, plus 1 extra tablespoon for dusting
50g cornflour

For the dipping sauce:
1 tablespoon light soy sauce
1 tablespoon water
½ teaspoon caster sugar
½ teaspoon finely grated fresh ginger

To fry:
600ml sunflower oil
1 teaspoon sesame oil
150g (approx.) assorted titbits — here are some ideas (but feel free to vary):
Peeled raw king prawns, tail on (approx. 60g)
Parboiled baby carrots (approx. 25g)
Strips or discs of courgette (approx. 25g)
Handful of shungiku and other herb leaves
Paper-thin fresh ginger slices
Paper-thin citrus slices
2 courgette flowers
Handful of other edible flowers, such as nasturtiums

To serve:
Small bowl of sea salt

Lactuca sativa

LETTUCES

Blank out memories of limp and lame leaves trapped in dreary sandwiches – proper lettuces offer character and crunch.

There are dozens of stunning varieties to explore. They range in leaf shape, texture and colour, from pink-speckled to a sultry dark red. Make the most of their diversity, mixing up your planting for visual effect.

Lettuces form the backbone of our salad supply as a cut-and-come-again crop – pluck off the outer leaves and let the plant regrow. The plants also don't mind light shade, so they are ideal for less sunny spots.

Experiment to find your favourites. Chef Heston Blumenthal once told me that he's a fan of the ultra-crisp 'Iceberg' lettuce, often vilified for its bland flavour.

Recommended varieties Distinguish between the different types of lettuce. Loose-leaf varieties do not develop tight hearts of leaves in the centre, so these are ideal for regular plucking of the outer leaves. 'Bronze Arrowhead', 'Lollo Rossa', 'Mottistone' and 'Freckles' are fine examples.

Cos lettuces, also known as Romaine, grow more upright, are crisper in texture and have better tolerance of hot weather. Try 'Lobjoits', 'Green Cos', 'Crisp Mint', 'Pinnokio', 'Black-seeded Simpson' and 'Little Gem'.

Crisphead lettuces are crunchy and mild-flavoured, and are best if you want to grow compact hearts. 'Iceberg' is the most famous example. 'Webb's Wonderful' and 'Reine de Glace' are other varieties to try. Superior flavour is found in the similar but slightly looser Batavian types, such as 'Grenoble Red' or the dark red 'Rosemoor'.

Butterhead lettuces have softer, waxy leaves and are prone to wilting. I grow fewer of these. Good examples are 'Marvel of Four Seasons' and 'Tom Thumb' For winter lettuce, go for hardy varieties such as 'Rouge D'Hiver', 'Reine de Glace', 'Lattuginho' and 'May King'.

Growing Lettuces are a cool-climate crop. Sow from early spring to early summer, avoiding the hottest months. Sow a new batch every two or three weeks for a constant supply. You can also sow suitable varieties in early autumn.

Either sow seed directly where the plants are to grow – sprinkle seed sparingly, to cut down on tedious thinning out later. Alternatively, sow

leaves · 5/5

into plug trays, two seeds per cell. Remove the weaker seedling once they have germinated, and plant out when they have at least one pair of sturdy leaves. *Spacing:* From around 10cm for baby leaf to 30cm for larger hearting lettuces. Allow 20cm between rows.

Containers *Minimum compost depth:* 10cm. Ideally use a soil-based compost, which retains more moisture, although multipurpose will do. Water regularly, taking care that the lettuces do not dry out. Lettuces are handy for filling gaps in larger containers. *Indoors:* It is tricky to grow sufficient quantities of lettuce in a small space.

In the ground Lettuces prefer a moist, light, fertile soil. Clear weeds and rake away any large stones and debris before sowing and planting.

Harvesting
In small spaces, it's best to grow lettuces as a cut-and-come-again crop, plucking off the outer leaves as needed. Hearting lettuces, however, should be cut in one go. If you need to perk up tired lettuce leaves, refresh in a bowl or sink of cold water for half an hour before drying and serving.

Seed saving
This is relatively easy, although there is a small possibility of cross-pollination between varieties. Allow the plant to flower and eventually white, tufty seeds will emerge. The seed ripens in stages, so harvest every few days, shaking or picking into a paper bag before drying.

Pests and diseases
Protect seedlings from slugs and snails. Moulds may be a problem in wet conditions. If plants suddenly wilt and die, it may indicate root aphids – uproot and dispose of affected plants.

Preserving
Best eaten fresh, as there is no satisfactory method.

Pluck off the outer leaves and allow the remainder to grow on

Notes
Lettuces are annuals in the Asteraceae (formerly Compositae) family, which includes chicory and endive.

Fast-growing, they are an excellent catch crop for filling in gaps or sowing in between other crops.

Keep well watered and mulched. Stressed plants start to shoot up and run to seed, which means the leaves become bitter.

Explore creative ways to plant – for example to edge a bed, or in stripes or circles.

In hot weather lettuces are prone to erratic germination. If you are determined to try, refrigerate seed for a day before planting and sow direct into their final growing positions late in the day, or in plug trays in a cool spot. Grow them on in light shade.

8 WAYS WITH LETTUCE

Lettuces are more about texture and colour than bold flavour. Mix up different leaf types for interest. To keep them in tiptop condition and minimise discoloration, tear or cut with a sharp knife at the last moment. Lettuces pair especially well with herbs and other intense flavours and dressings.

Salad dressings

❉ For a balsamic dressing, whisk one part balsamic vinegar with a generous pinch of salt, freshly ground pepper and a little mustard and honey. Then whisk again with three parts extra-virgin olive oil.

❉ For a lemony dressing, whisk one part freshly squeezed lemon juice and one part white wine vinegar with a generous pinch of salt and sugar. Then whisk again with three parts extra-virgin olive oil.

❉ For a blue cheese dressing, crumble the cheese into a bowl and then use a fork to mash and mix with just enough water to loosen. Whisk in freshly squeezed lemon juice, to taste, then season with salt and freshly ground pepper. Optional extras include a splash of sherry vinegar and chopped chives.

❉ For a summery dressing, whisk equal parts freshly squeezed orange juice and extra-virgin olive oil, then thicken, to taste, by whisking in white miso paste. I learnt this recipe from Chad Sarno, the great raw chef.

❉ For a gingery, Japanese-style dressing, whisk one part light soy sauce, one part rice wine vinegar, two parts mirin and three parts sunflower oil. Then add, to taste, finely grated fresh ginger, chopped spring onion and a few drops of toasted sesame oil.

❉ For a sweet sesame dressing, see page 23.

Other recipe ideas

❉ Use large lettuce leaves to make the tasty Korean-style wraps called *ssambap*. Prepare a selection of fillings, such as slow-cooked pork or slices of steak, cooked rice, herbs, sliced spring onions and chives. Pile the fillings into each lettuce leaf, add chilli sauce, then wrap and enjoy. For an authentic touch, buy a tub of *ssamjang*, the authentic chilli paste, to spice up your wraps. This is sold in oriental supermarkets.

❉ For a quick side dish, place chopped lettuce hearts and frozen peas in a pan with a knob of butter and splash of white wine or stock. Optional extras include diced shallot, bacon or cured ham. Simmer for 5 minutes or until cooked, season and serve.

PROPER VINAIGRETTE

A well-prepared salad dressing makes a world of difference, so here are step-by-step instructions for a classic vinaigrette – the sequence can also be applied to other dressing recipes. The key is to emulsify the dressing, which is when oil combines with vinegar, thickening it up. Either use a whisk and bowl or shake it hard in a lidded jam jar. I tend to do the latter, which is then easily stashed in the fridge. My standard ratio is one part vinegar to three parts oil, but adjust to taste.

Tip the salt into a small pile on a chopping board. Place the garlic on top. Use the flat side of a knife blade to smear and crush the garlic to a salty paste. Scoop the paste into a bowl or jar, then add the vinegar, pepper and sugar. Whisk or shake to dissolve. If using a whisk, gradually incorporate the olive oil to emulsify. If using a jam jar, add all the oil and shake hard. Allow the dressing to stand for a few minutes before serving.

Makes 200ml

1 teaspoon sea salt
¼ garlic clove
50ml red or white wine vinegar
Freshly ground black pepper
Pinch of caster sugar
150ml best extra-virgin olive oil

FRUIT

Fruits are all about temptation, designed to nourish the seed within and to be eaten, dispersed or whisked away to start a new life. Unlike the leaves, roots and stems, fruits rely on being consumed at a particular point in time – when ripe. So as a lure they often mature into an eye-catching bright colour and ripen with sugars to seduce the taste buds.

In this chapter I've included my favourite fruits for the urban grower, chosen because they suit smaller spaces. They are all examples of soft fruits, with stoneless soft flesh.

Bear in mind that these plants are perennials, with a life cycle of more than one year. Currants and gooseberries will be productive for well over ten years; strawberries for three. So they are an investment – plant them properly and they will save you effort in the long run.

Another option for a small space would be blueberries, which can be grown successfully outdoors in a large container filled with ericaceous (acidic) compost and should be watered with rainwater. For larger spaces, also try apples, blackcurrants, Japanese wineberries, loganberries, pears and raspberries, amongst others.

It's worth noting that some of the crops included elsewhere in this book are also technically a fruit. A fruit is the fertilised ovary of a plant, usually containing seeds. So chillies, courgettes, mouse melons, tomatoes, squashes and peas are all also the fruit of the plant.

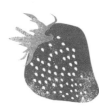

Fragaria x ananassa, F. vesca

STRAWBERRIES

Strawberries are a dream crop. The glorious, dangling, red fruits lift everyone's heart. But they are also a symbol of a modern malaise. Strawberries imported in December are fruit with no soul

Not long ago, their season was fleeting. Now they are available year-round and flavour has declined – along with our sense of anticipation.

Growing your own helps to put things right. So bring back the excitement with your own, personal strawberry season.

Recommended varieties Summer-fruiting strawberries are divided into early, mid- and late season. These crop heavily for a short period. Favourites include 'Royal Sovereign' (early), 'Cambridge Favourite' (mid) and 'Florence' (late).

Perpetual strawberries, also known as remontant or ever-bearers, are varieties that pump out fruit over many months, often with several bursts, from around mid-summer to late autumn. Their yield is lower, but it's a good idea to grow some of these to stretch the season. Favourites include 'Mara de Bois' and 'Albion'.

Wild and alpine varieties have distinct growing requirements and produce fewer, smaller fruit with intense flavour. They are an excellent choice for covering bare patches of your plot in partial shade, and will spread each year. They can be grown from seed. Alpines tend to produce no runners, but propagate by self-seeding. Try 'Alexandria' and 'Mignonette'.

Growing Ideally, grow a mixture of early, mid-, late and perpetual varieties to stretch your season. Buy plants or scrounge spares from friends. You can plant any time in the growing season, although spring or late summer is ideal. Choose a sunny position. Strawberries will also tolerate a little shade, but yield will be reduced. Prepare the planting hole, then spread out the roots as you plant the strawberry itself, taking care that the crown, the base of the plant, is at soil level. *Spacing:* Don't be tempted to cramp the plant as this can encourage moulds. Allow 30–45cm between individual plants, a little less for wild and alpine varieties. Allow 60–100cm between rows.

Containers *Minimum compost depth:* 20cm. Use a multipurpose compost, mixing in a few handfuls of garden compost, vermicompost or well-rotted

manure. Hanging baskets also work well. Growing bags should be raised off the ground with bricks or similar to deter pests.

When the plants are fruiting, it's a good idea to turn containers every few days to provide even exposure to the sun. Water regularly and use a general-purpose liquid feed, switching to a high-potassium feed once they start to flower and form fruit. *Indoors:* Not ideal, as pollination may be affected resulting in smaller and fewer fruit.

In the ground Strawberries prefer a rich, well-drained soil. Dig in plenty of well-rotted manure or garden compost a few weeks before planting. Chalky soils should be avoided. Sandy soils promote early crops. Heavier soils, such as loams and clays, encourage good flavour.

Harvesting

Pick when fully red and ripe, ideally still warm from the sun. Pinch off the fruits with a couple of centimetres of stalk.

Propagation

This is easily done via runners, new stems that creep laterally from the mother plant to form mini plantlets, and which then send out new roots. To propagate, peg the plantlets down into small pots filled with compost. Once they are anchored with roots, cut the plantlet away from the mother plant. This technique is handy for replenishing your patch with new plants or for trading with friends.

Pests and diseases

Birds, slugs and squirrels will eat the red fruit, so protect it with netting. Moulds and mildews can be a problem; for this reason, improve ventilation, water carefully and dispose of affected parts of plants (see page 165).

Preserving

Jams and conserves are the classic method of preserving strawberries, but you can also freeze them – mix with caster sugar, leave overnight, then freeze in a plastic container.

Notes

Strawberries are herbaceous perennials in the Rosaceae family, which includes apples and pears. They are self-fertile, although crops are improved by pollinating insects, such as honey bees, and by growing a group of strawberry plants together.

Strawberries are tough plants and will tolerate some neglect. They should be replaced every three or four years, and strawberry patches should be rotated around your plot.

To extend the season, provide extra heat and protection. For an early or late crop, you could grow under glass, for example in a greenhouse or cold frame. Alternatively, use a plastic cloche, such as a recycled plastic bottle (see page 160). Remove on sunny days to promote pollination.

If you can bear to wait, pick off the flowers from new plants in their first year to encourage a heavy crop in the next.

It is good practice to keep the fruit clean and prevent it from touching the soil or compost, as this can encourage pests and diseases. Some growers plant through slits in a sheet of plastic or water-permeable fabric. Or you can tuck straw underneath the fruit, removing it at the end of the growing season.

In autumn, prune summer-fruiting varieties back to about 7cm above the crown. With perpetuals, simply remove brown and old leaves.

6 WAYS WITH STRAWBERRIES

Strawberries are glorious whole, but it's also fun to mix up the textures by chopping them into halves, quarters or eighths, or even mashing them into a pulp. To enhance the flavour of the fruit, try sprinkling chopped strawberries with caster sugar and a few drops of balsamic or red wine vinegar or a squeeze of lemon juice. Strawberries go especially well with basil, green shiso, mint, yoghurt, ice cream, chocolate, other soft fruits and champagne.

❀ For a magnificent mixed fruit salad, marinate the fruit with a spiced sugar syrup. Dissolve sugar in an equal weight of water over a gentle heat, add spices (cardamom, cloves, cinnamon and ginger make a fine quartet) and simmer until reduced by half, finishing with a squeeze of lemon juice. Cool, strain and pour over the fruit. Try adding a few torn basil or green shiso leaves to the salad, too, before serving.

❀ Dip the fruits in chocolate. Chop good-quality chocolate into even-sized pieces, then melt in a heatproof bowl slotted over a saucepan of simmering water. Dip the strawberries in one by one, then place on greaseproof paper to cool and harden. You could also roll them into crushed nuts, dried coconut or sumac, a piquant red powder made from berries, especially popular in Lebanon and Syria.

❀ For a decadent treat, tip strawberries into a bowl, sprinkle with caster sugar and a few drops of balsamic or red wine vinegar, grate over orange and lime zest, then add a splash of champagne. Mix and marinate for half an hour.

❀ Try a salad of halved strawberries, feta cheese, avocado and green shiso or mint, with a balsamic salad dressing.

❀ For parties, thread cocktail sticks with strawberries, cut in half if large, and cubes of a rich chocolate brownie.

❀ Blend over-ripe or blemished fruit into smoothies or with yoghurt for an Indian lassi.

FLAMBÉED STRAWBERRIES

I once met a chap who ate strawberries for a living — he grew and tested new varieties. Unsurprisingly, he had many cunning recipes for the fruits such as this boozy treatment. To be honest, I was initially rather suspicious of cooking strawberries. But this recipe works a treat, as long as you use fresh fruit and cook fast, with maximum heat, so that the fruit barely softens. It should take little more than 1 minute once the butter has melted.

Flambéed strawberries are lovely served with ice cream, such as basil and lime (see page 94). I sometimes also add a twist of black pepper.

Serves 2–3

15g butter
1 tablespoon caster sugar
250g strawberries, halved
2 tablespoons Grand Marnier or brandy
Pinch of grated orange zest
Pinch of grated lemon zest
Mint leaves, to garnish

Melt the butter in a heavy-based frying pan or wok over a gentle heat. Add the sugar and stir to dissolve. Add the strawberries, stir, then pour in the alcohol and turn up the heat to high.

To flambé, carefully ignite the liquid with a match or lighter, or tip the pan to use the hob's gas flame. Allow the flames to die down, stir through the citrus zest, and let the juices bubble for a few seconds. Garnish with mint and eat immediately.

Ribes rubrum

REDCURRANTS & WHITECURRANTS

These are the crown jewels of fruit, in glistening whites, pinks and reds. Currants are beautiful and obliging, easy to grow in a garden, on a patio or in extra-large containers. As a bonus, they tolerate a touch of shade and keep going for a decade or more. White and pink varieties are especially desirable – near impossible to buy, and deeply delicious.

Blackcurrants are not included here because they grow and are pruned in different ways. They also need more sun to ripen fully. But don't let that put you off. They are also a terrific crop, and the recipes here suit them too.

Recommended varieties For redcurrants, you can find early, mid- and late season varieties such as 'Jonkheer Van Tets', 'Laxton's No.1' and 'Redstart', respectively. The fruit from white- and pinkcurrants tends to be smaller and sweeter, but you won't find a huge selection of varieties, even in specialist nurseries: 'Blanka' and 'Versailles' are the main varieties of white; 'Gloire de Sablon' of pink.

Growing Don't expect a large harvest for the first year or two. Buy two- or three-year-old bare-root plants, perhaps in a trained shape if available, in the same way as for gooseberries (see page 134).

Ideally choose a sunny position, although currants will also tolerate a touch of shade. Ensure the site has decent air circulation and shelter from cold winds. Currants do not thrive in exposed positions such as a rooftop. *Spacing:* About 1.5m for bushes; 40cm for cordons. They can grow over 1m in height.

Containers *Minimum compost depth:* 60cm. Growing currants is possible in a large container, with a minimum diameter of 50cm, filled with a soil-based compost. Bush shapes are best suited to pots. Add a slow-release general-purpose fertiliser when planting. Water well and regularly, whenever the soil surface is dry, until water drains out of the bottom of the container. Repot each winter, moving into a slightly larger pot in readiness for spring. *Indoors:* Not suitable.

In the ground Prepare the ground well, removing any perennial weeds. Currants cope with most soils but need good drainage. Follow the nursery's planting instructions. Mulch as for gooseberries.

fruit   2/5

Harvesting Currants grow in strigs, which are cascades of fruit dangling off a slender stalk. Snip off individual strigs when the fruit is dry, shiny, fully ripe and bright in colour. You can then use a fork to strip the fruit from the stalk.

Propagation Raise new plants from hardwood cuttings taken in autumn (see page 179). These are easier to root than gooseberries.

Preserving Pick the fruit when dry. Currants freeze well using the open-tray technique (see page 182) before bagging up. Alternatively, purée with caster sugar and freeze, or preserve with brandy (see overleaf). Currants contain decent amounts of pectin so are excellent for jams and jellies.

Pests and diseases Blistered leaves and pale green insects indicate currant blister aphid, but the damage is cosmetic. Defoliation may indicate sawfly caterpillars: check in the centre of the bush for the first signs of damage and pick them off.

Notes

Currants are deciduous shrubs in the Grossulariaceae family, which includes gooseberries. They are largely self-fertile, although pollination is improved by insects.

Water well during dry periods, especially when the plant is forming fruit.

Be aware that currants have shallow roots, so take care if cultivating and weeding the surrounding soil.

5 WAYS WITH CURRANTS

Mix up the reds, pinks and whites. Serve on the strig or scatter individual currants. They pair especially well with basil, lemon verbena, mint, rosemary, cloves, lamb and venison.

❀ Add fresh currants to a sponge pudding (see page 139), use in sorbets, add to sponges for cupcakes, suspend in jellies, or simmer down for a fruit sauce for a soufflé (see page 145).

❀ For a quick chocolate sauce for ice cream, simmer a handful of currants with 1 tablespoon each of sugar and water, grate in chocolate, allow to melt and serve.

❀ For a simple redcurrant sauce for roasted meat, sauté a diced shallot in butter, then add fresh redcurrants, a dollop of redcurrant jelly, port wine and orange zest. Reduce to the consistency you like, season and serve. You can also add currants to other rich sauces to lend a fruity acidity.

❀ Perk up shop-bought redcurrant jelly by warming slightly then mashing in fresh redcurrants.

❀ To frost currants with sugar, beat an egg white in a bowl then use a pastry brush to paint this onto whole strigs or individual currants before rolling them in a bowl of icing or caster sugar. These make exquisite decoration for cakes and tarts.

BRANDIED CURRANTS

Makes 1 large jar

200g blemish-free currants
250ml brandy
7 tablespoons granulated sugar
2 tablespoons water

In San Francisco, the Zuni Café has long been flying the flag for seasonal, locally grown produce. This method of preserving currants comes from the chef Judy Rodgers' terrific The Zuni Café Cookbook. *I like the simple way that you can preserve whole strigs of currants, capturing their beauty. When serving, fish the currant strigs out from the jar an hour ahead. They are lovely with pâté, lamb chops or posh sausage and mash.*

Choose a sterilised jar that will accommodate the currants (see page 184). Wash then dry the currants on a clean tea towel and pack the fruit into the jar. Pour the brandy into a bowl or pan, add the sugar, stir well to dissolve, then add the water. Pour this liquid over the currants. Seal the jar, tapping to remove any air bubbles. Store in a cool, dark place for 1 week and then transfer to the fridge.

Ribes uva-crispa

GOOSEBERRIES

Of all the soft fruits, gooseberries are my favourite. They are much underrated and should be more widely grown,

Gooseberries are tough, long-lasting plants that are tolerant of light shade and their fruit is the first of the season. They are ideal in back gardens and can be grown in large containers. Of the dozens of varieties, the rare purple fruits are particularly fine.

The fruit was once much more popular than it is today, especially in Britain. But in recent years it has been usurped by the blueberry – a blander fruit with savvier marketing. Gooseberries sold in shops tend to be picked early and are therefore tart. Properly ripe, however, the fruits are a sublime balance of sweetness and acidity.

Recommended varieties If you have space, choose early, mid- and late season varieties to stretch the season. Definitely include a red or purple variety, such as 'Pax' (mid), 'Martlet' (mid to late), 'London' (mid) and 'Hinnomaki Red' (mid). Reliable yellow gooseberries include 'Leveller' (late). Tasty green varieties include 'Invicta' (early) and 'Whitesmith' (mid).

Growing Bear in mind that your harvest will be modest for the first year or two. Buy two- or three-year-old bare-root plants from specialist fruit nurseries in autumn or winter. These are plants that have gone dormant, and can therefore be sent in the post without a pot. They are significantly less expensive than plants sold growing in containers.

The bush is the standard shape of a gooseberry plant, but if other shapes of trained plants are available match them to your growing space: a fan might work well against a wall, for example; an upright cordon, which has a single main stem, would work well in small spaces. Half-standards are bush-shaped plants on a long stem, around a metre in height, and make an eye-catching feature for gardens or large containers. *Spacing:* About 1.5m for bushes; 30cm for cordons; 1m for fans. They can grow over 1m in height.

fruit   2/5

Containers *Minimum compost depth:* 60cm. It is possible to grow gooseberries in a large container, with a minimum diameter of 50cm, filled with a soil-based compost. Bushes or half-standards are best suited to containers. Add a slow-release general-purpose fertiliser when planting. Water well and regularly whenever the soil surface is dry, until water drains out of the bottom of the container. Repot each winter, moving into a slightly larger pot in readiness for spring. *Indoors:* Not suitable.

In the ground Gooseberries are happiest in the ground and are not fussy about soil type. Choose a sheltered position in full sun or light shade and plant according to the nursery's instructions. Pull off, rather than cut, any new side shoots from the bottom 10cm of the plant stem. Spread a 5cm layer of mulch around the base of the plant, using garden compost, composted bark chips or similar to retain moisture and suppress weeds. Feed with a general-purpose fertiliser in spring.

Harvesting A squeeze and taste will reveal their degree of ripeness. The first, smaller fruit are more tart and best used for cooking.

Propagation Raise new plants from hardwood cuttings taken in autumn (see page 179).

Pests and diseases Birds may eat the ripe fruit: drape the bush with netting or grow in a fruit cage. A powdery, greyish white fungus on stems, leaves and fruit indicates American gooseberry mildew. Remove affected bits of plant and improve air circulation. Defoliation may indicate sawfly caterpillars: check in the centre of the bush for the first signs of damage and pick them off.

Preserving The fruit freezes well using the open-tray method (see page 182). Alternatively, simmer with sugar until the skin bursts, sieve, then allow the syrup to cool before freezing in ice-cube trays or freezer bags. You can also use gooseberries in relishes and chutneys. Gooseberries are rich in pectin for jam- and jelly-making.

Notes

Gooseberries are woody perennials in the Grossulariaceae family, which includes currants. They have a productive life of well over ten years and are the deepest-rooting of the soft fruit.

Fewer varieties are available these days – around 300 were grown in Britain in the nineteenth century.

If the plant is producing a heavy crop, thin the fruits before they begin to ripen, removing at least every other fruit. This encourages the remainder to reach full size.

Gooseberries like to be kept moist; don't allow them to dry out in hot weather.

4 WAYS WITH GOOSEBERRIES

Top and tail first if serving the fruit whole. Gooseberries combine especially well with fresh root or preserved stem ginger, lemongrass, rhubarb, star anise, and foraged elderflower and sweet cicely.

❀ Make a simple sauce for oily fish such as mackerel. Gently melt a knob of butter in a saucepan. Rinse and drain the prepared fruit, then add it, still dripping, to the pan. Cook until soft, mash with a fork, then stir in brown sugar to taste and then season. I also like to add a touch of chopped fresh ginger or nutmeg. You can sieve the sauce if you are fussy about pips, or add a splash of double cream for a touch of luxury.

❀ Roast whole fruit with brown sugar for an instant jam. Spread on toast or croissants or stir through yoghurt for breakfast or a quick pudding. Preheat the oven to 150°c/300°F/gas 2. Wash the fruit, tip it onto a baking tray, mix with brown sugar and roast for 10 minutes or until starting to caramelise. Try this with rhubarb, too.

❀ Use the fruit in compotes and crumbles. Try stewing in elderflower cordial. Or – an idea from chef Richard Corrigan – bake a pie with a filling of gooseberries and sorrel leaves, with sugar to sweeten.

❀ Play around with using sweeter gooseberries in mixed salads, perhaps pairing with basil or fennel.

GOOSEBERRY ICE CREAM

Serves 4

450g gooseberries
110g caster sugar
140ml double cream

My friends Tim and Alison grow their gooseberries on Spanish hills, looking out over the dairy country of Cantabria. They swear by this recipe, adapted from Elizabeth David's book Summer Cooking. *It is rich and delicious. Tarter gooseberries are best here, so you are safe to top up with shop-bought fruit if necessary.*

Put the gooseberries and sugar in a pan with 1 tablespoon of water. Simmer gently, covered, until soft. Strain through a sieve, taking care to scrape off precious pulp from the bottom of the sieve. Taste the purée to check the sweetness, adding more sugar if needed. When cold, mix with the double cream. Churn and freeze in an ice-cream maker. Alternatively, freeze in a plastic container and churn by hand (see basil ice cream recipe, page 94).

STICKY SPONGE PUDDING

This gorgeous, old-school pud is a versatile recipe to have up your sleeve. For a dramatic touch, lift up the pudding basin at table to reveal the steaming, treacly fruit. You will need a pudding basin, a pan with lid large enough for it to sit in, a sieve, greaseproof paper, kitchen foil, scissors and string.

I also make this pudding in the cooler months with defrosted gooseberries from the freezer. To vary the base, toss in redcurrants or blueberries for colour. You could also ditch the gooseberries and use just golden syrup, marmalade, jam, tinned peaches or pineapple, or dried fruit soaked first in some booze — perhaps rum or brandy.

Serve with ice cream, crème fraîche or crème anglaise.

Serves 4

For the base:
Large handful of gooseberries, topped and tailed
4 tablespoons golden syrup

For the sponge:
110g unsalted butter, chopped into cubes and at room temperature
110g caster sugar
Zest of 1 lime
2 eggs
110g self-raising flour
1 teaspoon baking powder
Pinch of ground ginger
50ml full-fat milk (approx.)

Grease a pudding basin, about 1.2–1.9 litres in volume, with a little butter. Add the gooseberries and pour over the syrup to cover the base. (If using frozen fruit, defrost and dry in a clean tea towel before adding.)

In a mixing bowl, beat together the 110g of butter and sugar until light, fluffy and almost white. This will take about 10 minutes with a spatula or fork, or 5 minutes with an electric mixer. Mix in the lime zest. Using a whisk, beat in the eggs one at a time.

Sift in the flour, baking powder and ground ginger, then fold them into the mixture using a spatula. Stir in the milk bit by bit, adding just enough to loosen the mixture's consistency until it drops happily from a spoon. Pour the mixture over the syrupy gooseberries and level with the back of the spoon.

Make a cover for the pudding to exclude steam and water. Cut a square of greaseproof paper that will generously cover the top of the pudding basin. Then cut an equal-sized square of kitchen foil and place this on top. Fold a central pleat, around 3cm in width, to allow for expansion if the pudding rises above the basin. Lay this over the top of the basin with the foil facing upwards. Push down the edges, then fasten the string below the rim of the pudding basin, using a knot to secure. Trim the edges of the cover to neaten.

Steam for 2-2½ hours, covered, in a large pan of simmering water. The water should reach no more than halfway up the basin. Top up the water during the cooking process if necessary.

To serve, run a knife around the edge of the pudding, cover the bowl with a plate and flip. Pour over more golden syrup if you fancy.

FLOWERS

All flowers deserve a place in the veg patch, adding a splash of colour and livening up the plot. The most useful flowers to grow are those that are not only ravishing, but also edible.

Most edible flowers have a subtle or little flavour – they are all about eating with your eyes. This is not surprising when you consider the botany. Plants produce flowers to attract bees and other pollinating insects to their reproductive organs – the colourful petals are designed to lure and entice rather than to feed. As I write, in fact, bumblebees are stuffing their fat bodies into the cascades of red nasturtiums outside my window.

There are some notable exceptions, such as nasturtiums, whose flowers have a distinctive, peppery flavour. The squash family, including courgettes and winter squashes, has flowers with a gentle but beguiling taste. Marigolds, chamomile and day lilies are among others to try. I also adore borage, although the plants grow tall and are tricky in small spaces.

Pick edible flowers when young and at their best, and, if in doubt, eat only the petals. Peek inside first, to check for insects. Avoid rinsing, as it makes them soggy.

Tropaeolum majus
NASTURTIUMS

Of the many edible flowers, nasturtiums win by a mile. Their flavour is distinct and delicious, intense and peppery. You can also eat the leaves, flower buds and seeds.

I admire their idiosyncratic style. Their strange, lily-pad leaves evoke an otherworldly feel. The plants also thrive on neglect. What more could you ask for? No plot is complete without nasturtiums.

Recommended varieties There is a wide choice of compact, trailing and white-streaked, variegated varieties, with single or double flowers. All taste much the same. Match your choice to your growing space: trailing varieties, for example, will flow over the sides of a container.

Flower colour ranges from pastel shades to deep reds. I prefer darker shades and non-variegated leaves. Try 'Empress of India', 'Tip Top Mahogany' and 'Black Velvet'. You may also find rarer, perennial forms of nasturtium such as 'Machua'. These vigorous climbers are harder to cultivate and are traditionally grown for their tubers.

Growing Nasturtiums are easy to grow. They flower more profusely in a sunny position. In spring, sow seed in plug trays, one seed per cell, or into small pots, then plant out the seedlings. Alternatively, sow direct in the spot where you want them to flower. Water if very dry, but never feed. *Spacing:* About 20cm between plants.

Containers *Minimum compost depth:* 15cm. Aim for a low-nutrient mix so avoid using fresh multipurpose compost if possible. Recycle compost from pots, mix up the dregs from old bags of compost or use garden compost, which is generally lower in nutrients than the shop-bought sort. Trailing nasturtiums are fantastic for dangling over the sides of hanging baskets and window boxes, or for edging and disguising containers. Try mingling with tomatoes. *Indoors:* Compact varieties of nasturtium can be grown as houseplants, although it seems a shame that their flowers will not be enjoyed by flying insects such as bumblebees.

In the ground Nasturtiums do best in poor, free-draining soil. A rich soil will produce large leaves but few flowers.

flowers, leaves, seeds — 5/5

Harvesting Harvest the leaves, flower buds, flowers and seeds throughout their long season. Always pick flowers when prime and perky as they are less appetising once faded. Seeds are best when green, tender and smaller than a chickpea.

Seed saving This is easy. Nasturtiums happily self-seed. To collect, gather the larger, ripe seeds before they drop or rot, then dry and store.

Pests and diseases Blackfly targets nasturtiums. Dispose of heavily affected parts (see page 163).

Preserving Mix the flowers with butter, lemon zest and sea salt for freezing, or freeze whole flowers in ice-cubes (see page 182). At the end of the season, preserve the leaves and flowers in a pesto (see page 92). Young buds and seeds can be pickled, but are not really worth the bother.

Notes

Nasturtiums can be either annuals or perennials from the *Tropaeolum* genus, native to Peru. They were a favourite of the Aztecs, with the first species brought to Europe by Spanish conquistadores.

Nasturtiums flower over a long period, but succumb to the first hard frosts. Pick off dead or dying flowers throughout their season.

6 WAYS WITH NASTURTIUMS

The flowers are the prime harvest. Check inside for insects, shaking any out, and do not wash or rinse as it makes the flowers soggy. The leaves are also delicious but more pungent. The buds and seeds contain tiny amounts of oxalic acid, a natural substance that is harmful in large quantities, so eat only small amounts. Nasturtiums combine well with basil, dill, tomatoes, eggs and creamy cheeses.

❀ For salads, use both the flowers and the leaves, torn into bits if you feel the flavour is too strong. Balance with milder leaves such as lettuce and purslane. Add flowers after any salad dressing to keep the petals dry.

❀ Add the flowers and leaves to sandwiches. (I love them in an egg mayonnaise sandwich, also stuffed with a few crisps for crunch.) Or try a nasturtium-flower sandwich on white sliced bread with salted butter.

❀ Float the lily-pad leaves in soups.

❀ Mix the leaves, flowers and buds into a pesto, either on their own or with other herbs such as mint and basil (see page 92).

❀ Use the flowers and leaves in a tempura (see page 119), Vietnamese summer rolls (see page 88), or use large leaves in place of lettuce for Korean-style wraps (see page 122).

❀ Scatter the caper-like young flower buds over pizza.

NASTURTIUM SOUFFLÉ

This is a saucy soufflé for two, laced with nasturtium petals for colour and a subtle, peppery kick. Soufflés look impressive, but aren't that difficult once you get the hang of the basic technique. The magical rise is created by the heat of the oven, which causes expansion of water vapour and air in the egg-white bubbles.

Use ramekins or any round, ovenproof dishes, preferably with straight sides. Choose two the same size or make one larger soufflé to share.

You can also easily scale up this recipe or adapt the flavouring. Try savoury versions with chervil, dill, sorrel or chives. Or sweet soufflés made with a chocolate or redcurrant sauce. This soufflé is best served with a green salad, decorated with more nasturtium flowers.

Position a baking tray in the top half of your oven. This will help your soufflés to rise. Preheat the oven to 200°c/400°f/gas 6.

Grease two ramekins, around 9cm in diameter, with butter. Sprinkle the buttered sides with a little Parmesan.

In a heavy saucepan, melt the butter over a low heat. Slowly sift in the flour, stirring as you go. Add the cayenne pepper and cook for 1 minute. Gradually add the milk, using a whisk to mix together, and then bring the sauce to a gentle bubble for 2–3 minutes, or until it thickens. Turn off the heat, then allow to cool for 1 minute.

Beat the egg yolks well with a fork, then whisk them into the sauce. Add the grated strong cheese and stir until it melts from the residual heat. Taste and season generously with salt and pepper – you want a strong flavour.

Using an electric or balloon whisk, whisk the egg whites in a clean bowl until they form soft, glossy peaks that hold their shape. Take care to do it properly – otherwise the soufflé will struggle to rise. It may take up to 5 or more minutes if whisking by hand.

Add a dollop of whisked egg white to the pan and stir to loosen the cheesy mixture. Gently pour this mixture over the egg white in the bowl, add the nasturtium petals, then fold slowly together with a spatula. Aim to keep the air bubbles intact, and move the spatula in a slow, downward motion through the mix, curving back out of the bowl.

Pour the mixture into the ramekins until two-thirds full. Run your finger around the edge of the mixture in the ramekins – this helps the soufflés to rise. Sprinkle some extra Parmesan on top.

Place the ramekins on the preheated baking tray and bake for 10–12 minutes, or until the soufflés are risen and brown on top. (If making one soufflé to share, this may take around twice as long to cook.) Avoid opening the oven door if you can. Eat swiftly, before they gracefully deflate.

Serves 2, as a starter or light main course

20g butter, plus extra for greasing
2 teaspoons finely grated Parmesan cheese, for lining the ramekins and for topping
15g plain flour
Pinch of cayenne pepper
150ml full-fat milk
2 eggs, separated
80g strong cheese, finely grated (I like a mix of Gruyère and Parmesan)
Salt and freshly ground black pepper
Large handful of nasturtium petals, preferably red

Viola tricolor

VIOLAS

Violas are a blessing – small, tough plants that offer splashes of colour over many months. They gently parade their dainty, edible flowers from spring to autumn. Dot them around your plot and kitchen plates.

The flowers are stunning, but, unlike nasturtiums, have little taste. Think of them as eye candy. The tricoloured wild viola, commonly known as heartsease, is the most widely available but there are dozens of other varieties to explore. I have half a dozen in pots and edging my raised beds, and pick the flowers to brighten up special meals.

Recommended varieties Heartsease (*Viola tricolor*) is an excellent choice for colour and for growing from seed. Most other varieties are derived from this plant. 'Molly Sanderson' and 'Bowles Black' have chic black petals. Some are scented, such as 'Cinders'; others, such as 'Delphine', have a more trailing habit useful for containers. Your best bet is to find a specialist nursery and browse their catalogue. Do not confuse African violets (*Saintpaulia*) with violas – these are unrelated and not edible.

Growing Violas will get by in partial shade, but will flower more profusely in full sun. Just a handful of varieties are available as seed. Sow from early spring to mid-summer, direct in the ground or in plug trays, one seed per cell, to plant out later. Alternatively, specialist nurseries supply a wide range of established plants from spring to mid-summer. Once you have planted them, snip off any flowers and buds that are about to flower, as this focuses the plant's energy on growing a strong root system. *Spacing:* About 25cm between plants.

Containers *Minimum compost depth:* 25cm. Violas do well in containers. Varieties with a more trailing habit are excellent for hanging baskets. Combine them with other crops to add colour. Use a soil-based compost mix, ideally adding a few handfuls of grit for drainage and a slow-release general-purpose fertiliser. During the growing season, alternate between a general-purpose liquid feed and a high-potassium feed for best results. *Indoors:* Violas are better suited to the cooler conditions outside, so should not be kept indoors.

In the ground Violas prefer fertile soil and will grow in small clumps.

flowers · 5/5

They are useful for squeezing into gaps around your plot – for example, between paving stones on a path.

Harvesting Snip off the flowers. Violas are also wonderful cut flowers, arranged in small vases.

Pests and diseases Small field slugs can target the flower buds. If you notice damage, check the leaves and pick them off. Aphids and mildew can occasionally cause problems (see pages 163, 165).

Preserving You can crystallise viola flowers with egg white and caster sugar, but it is a fiddly process. The best way is to freeze whole flowers in ice cubes (see page 182).

Propagation Tease out stems from the base of the plant. Some may already have roots. Place into a cutting mix (see page 179) and plant out once the cuttings have developed a healthy root system.

Notes

Violas are hardy annuals and perennials in the Violaceae family. This includes pansies, which tend to produce larger flowers, and scented sweet violets and wood violets.

Always deadhead tired flowers by picking or cutting them off.

At the end of the season, once the flowers die down, cut off the flowering stems and old growth, leaving just the newer growth towards the base of the plant. Spread a few handfuls of fresh shop-bought or garden compost around the plant and allow to rest over winter.

Viola 'Bowles Black' flourishing in a windowbox

WAYS WITH VIOLAS

I don't cook with violas or do anything fancy. They are for colour, not flavour, so the only limit is your imagination. Add at the last moment to decorate fruit or savoury salads, for example, or pop viola ice cubes (see page 182) into a cool gin and tonic or sparkling cordial.

AFGHAN RICE PUDDING

Serves 6

120g pudding or round rice
500ml cold water
200ml full-fat milk
100ml double cream
4 cardamom pods
60g caster sugar
2 teaspoons rosewater
30g unsalted raw pistachios,
  finely chopped
6 viola flowers

Colourful violas add the finishing touch to this favourite pudding, lifted by the exotic flavours of cardamom and rosewater. I found the original recipe in the late Jeremy Round's excellent book The Independent Cook. *My version is less sweet and rich, but still deeply luxurious. Think dainty and serve in small dishes with a teaspoon.*

Place the rice and water in a medium-sized pan with a lid. Bring to the boil, covered, over medium heat. Then remove the lid and simmer gently until the water has all but evaporated, stirring now and then to prevent sticking. This will take about 15–20 minutes.

Stir in the milk and cream. Simmer, uncovered, for a further 15 minutes, or until the pudding is of a consistency you prefer. Stir regularly to prevent sticking.

Crush the cardamom pods using a pestle and mortar or similar. Discard the husks, then crush the black inner seeds to a powder. Add this powder and the sugar to the rice, stir, and cook for 2 minutes.

Remove the pan from the heat, allow to cool slightly, then stir in the rosewater. Spoon into individual small bowls and sprinkle the pistachios in a circle on top, placing a viola in the centre. Serve warm, not hot.

EXTRAS

152 **EGGS**

156 **HONEY**

Both chickens and bees can live happily in the city, which means our urban harvest can stretch beyond plants.

I've kept chickens for years and they are remarkably hassle-free. Gathering their fresh eggs is a daily treat. The key issue, of course, is space. I have seen hens kept on a rooftop but have my doubts. Chickens love to scratch around so are more content on open ground such as a back garden or allotment. I remember a particularly happy moment from last summer — hens sunbathing on a warm compost heap that was stuffed with worms, lazily slurping them up like spaghetti. Now that was a vision of true happiness.

Beekeeping is a more demanding hobby, but their honey is the ultimate urban crop. Bees actually prefer the diverse forage of city gardens, parks and wild corners over the monocultures of much modern countryside. A hive can thrive in all manner of sites, from rooftops to patios, but you need shelter from strong winds and easy access. If the hive is close to human traffic, netting or a wall of plants will encourage a flight path above head height. Observing bees at work is a great pleasure — both fascinating and relaxing.

EGGS

I'm not soppy about my hens. I don't give them pet names or stroke them on my lap. In fact, I frequently curse or chase my chickens as they trash yet another prized plant. Nevertheless, I am a huge fan of keeping poultry. I love their feisty character as much as their gift of fresh eggs. My two hens keep me company when I garden, rooting around beside me and gobbling up worms, slugs and snails. They polish off my kitchen scraps. And, to be honest, I do have a picture of my very first chicken, Betty, on the mantelpiece – she was a legend.

When buying the chickens themselves, your first choice is between hybrids and fancy pure breeds. Hybrids lay more eggs and are cheaper, although less glamorous. Ex-battery chickens are hybrid hens. Pure breeds have all the looks but are often less regular layers. Keep at least two hens, as one will get lonely. You do not need a cockerel, as hens will happily lay without their attentions. You will find adverts for poultry breeders in the back of country lifestyle or smallholder magazines. Select active birds with shiny feathers and a bright red comb.

Chickens should lay one egg almost every day, although bouts of hot or cold weather may put them off their stride. Some lay eggs of unusual colours, such as lovely pastel greens, blues and speckled dark browns. Hens also decline in productivity as they get older. Eggs keep for a long time – around a fortnight in cool temperatures, so there's little need to store them in the fridge. Just develop a system to eat your eggs in order of freshness.

4 WAYS WITH EGGS

To test if an egg is fresh, place it in a glass of water: fresh eggs sink and lie horizontal; old eggs will float upright, wide-end first. Cracking the egg provides other clues – pert, fresh yolks flatten with age. Note that the shell is porous, so eggs can absorb strong flavours nearby. Eggs combine especially well with chives, sorrel, bacon, chilli, tomatoes and truffles.

* For perfect soft-boiled eggs, I use a spoon to lower each egg into simmering water and set a timer – 4¾ minutes is spot-on for eggs from my chickens. Hard-boiled eggs take 7 minutes, and should be cooled under running water before peeling. Of course, there are other clever methods, but these work fine for me.
* For a perfect fried egg, fry a fresh egg in butter over a low to medium heat, using a spoon to baste the top of the egg with the fat. Before serving, a light sprinkle of paprika adds a colourful touch.
* For perfect scrambled eggs, melt a little butter in a heavy-based pan, break in the eggs, stir to mix lightly and rupture the yolks, then cook over a low heat, stirring gently every 5 seconds or so. Halfway through, season with salt and pepper, adding an optional touch of crème fraîche for a bit of luxury. Remove the eggs from the heat before they are quite ready, allowing them time to cook further on the plate. For a spicy alternative, try scrambled eggs Mexican style with onion, tomato, green chilli and coriander.
* Use eggs in savoury or sweet soufflés (see page 145), or in other classic egg dishes such as frittatas, tortillas and omelettes. Meringues, custards and cakes are sweet favourites.

AIOLI

What's the difference between aioli and mayonnaise? Not much. Both are an emulsion of egg and oil, made with a similar method. Aioli, however, always includes olive oil and garlic; mayonnaise is much less fussy.

This recipe is for aioli – divine with roast potatoes, grilled red meat or fish, or as a dip for veg and toasted bread. It will keep for three days, sealed, in the fridge.

To make either, you will need a balloon whisk or food processor. Eggs and oil should be at room temperature. Once the basic method is mastered, there are infinite variations. Add other ingredients to the base such as mustard, paprika, harissa, wasabi or anchovy. Switch fresh garlic for sweeter roasted garlic. Experiment with different oils – rapeseed, for example, lends a golden colour. You can also mix in chopped herbs, capers or gherkins just before serving.

Place the garlic cloves on a chopping board. Using the flat side of a knife, bash the cloves and remove the skin. Sprinkle the salt on the chopping board, place the bashed cloves on top, then use the sharp side of the knife to smear, not chop, the garlic into a smooth, salty paste. Scoop up the paste with the knife and place in a bowl. Add a squeeze of lemon juice and the egg yolks, then whisk to mix. Start adding the oil very gradually, drop by drop, whisking constantly to combine and emulsify. Once you have successfully incorporated a quarter of the oil, you can speed up. When all the oil has been added, taste the aioli, adding more salt or lemon juice as needed.

Serves 4

3 garlic cloves
½ teaspoon sea salt
Lemon juice, to taste
2 egg yolks
200ml oil (equal parts olive and sunflower oil)

HONEY

Keeping bees is a fascinating experience but not for the faint hearted. It demands both commitment and patience. I learnt the hard way. My first attempts were embarrassingly inept: losing swarms; angry bees in my trousers; or spilling sugar syrup over my hive while under attack from every neighbourhood wasp. The rewards, however, are sweet. Bees are also crucial pollinators for your local area.

It is a great pleasure to observe bees at work. The queen bee, pictured here with the white mark, looks quite different from the other bees. She is larger with a long, slender body. The queen bee is the reproductive organ of the colony, responsible for laying eggs. The rest of the hive consists of female workers, who do the bulk of the work, and a small number of male drones who mate with virgin queens.

Bees love the city as there is such a wide diversity of forage. Their honey harvest, however, is something of a gamble. Some years will produce a bumper crop of up to 40kg per hive. In other years they may produce very little. Urban honey is known for its superior, complex flavour and yours will be a unique distillation of the floral character of your neighbourhood. It is a brilliant gift for friends and any surplus will fetch a good price.

6 WAYS WITH HONEY

Honey is a sweetener but has a more complex flavour than processed sugars. Moreover, different honeys possess varied characters and colour depending on the floral season. A dark autumn honey, for example, is more strongly flavoured than a wildflower honey from mid-summer.

Honey will last forever. It is a natural preservative – the Romans used it to preserve fruits. When cooking, note that honey is approximately 25 per cent sweeter than sugar, so adjust measures accordingly. Also note that a jar of honey that has set hard will return to a runny state if placed in a bowl of hot water. Honey combines especially well with most herbs and spices, ginger, nuts, citrus and tart fruits such as gooseberries and rhubarb.

❁ Create a simple Asian marinade for chicken, pork or salmon by mixing equal quantities of honey and soy sauce and finely chopped fresh ginger and garlic, adjusting to taste. A touch of citrus zest and juice will sharpen up the flavour.

❁ Use honey as a glaze for fruits, vegetables and meats. For example, brush over halved plums to flash-grill or over root vegetables for roasting or mix with lemon juice, olive oil and thyme to slather over chicken thighs before cooking in the oven.

❁ Trickle over cheeses, such as a plate of fresh goat's cheese, ripe figs, walnuts and mint leaves.

❁ Add a little honey to salad dressings, in place of a pinch of sugar (see page 122).

❁ Stir honey into smoothies or herbal teas – try with a hot infusion of basil and ginger, or mint and lemon.

❁ Casseroles, stews, marinades and dark sauces often benefit from a little honey. Add with discretion, tasting as you go. You could add spices to a jar of honey to devote exclusively to cooking. Try cinnamon, cloves, coriander seeds, bay leaves and a sprig of rosemary.

HONEY & BASIL DAIQUIRI

My favourite summer sharpener is from a recipe by cocktail maestro Simon Difford of Difford's Guide. *Use a golden Caribbean or white Cuban rum. The quantities given are for one cocktail – scale up as necessary. Serve in a Martini glass or similar.*

First, chill your glass. Fill with ice cubes and set aside.

Add all the remaining ingredients to a cocktail shaker, in the order listed. Fill with ice cubes. Shake hard for 15 seconds. Tip out the ice from the chilled glass, then strain in the daiquiri.

Serves 1

Ice cubes
25ml fresh lime juice
1 tablespoon runny honey
10–12 medium basil leaves, torn
50ml golden or white rum

PESTS & DISEASES

At some point, it's bound to happen – your plants will get eaten or fall ill. Some of the culprits are obvious, such as slugs, cats or squirrels. Others are more mysterious, from strange moulds to a mystery virus.

The brutal truth is that there's a myriad of possible pests, diseases and disorders lurking out there. Fortunately, you are unlikely to encounter the vast majority.

For this reason, I'm keeping this section simple, summarising the most common problems you are likely to find – the usual suspects and their symptoms and cures. If your malady is not covered, a quick bit of online research should point you in the right direction.

It's worth repeating the mantra that prevention is always better than cure. Healthy plants, like humans, have strong immune systems. Weak and flimsy plants, overfed and grown too fast, are more likely to succumb. So strive to grow vigorous, tough plants – it will save you time and frustration in the long run.

Slugs and snails

Symptoms: irregular holes in leaves; decimated seedlings, sometimes eaten right through at the stem.

There are dozens of species of slugs and snails, and most are helpful – gently breaking down garden waste. But the nasty ones can wreak serious damage.

The two molluscs are related, but there are key differences: slugs often leave a continuous slime trail, which offers a useful clue to their attacks, and some species live underground, out of sight; snails are superior climbers and also leave a slime trail but it may be more spotted than continuous. Both tend to feed in moist conditions and after dark, so grab a torch one night and patrol your plot – it can be an eye-opener as to the extent of your problem.

In general, aim to keep populations down as you will never eliminate every slug and snail. Also try to deploy a combination of strategies, rather than relying on just one approach.

Disposing of slugs and snails is a dilemma for your conscience. Snip them in half and leave as food for the wildlife. Or, if you are squeamish, liberate them elsewhere: choose an unloved spot, which offers some plants for food, at least 100m away from your plot. I throw mine as snacks for my chickens.

❀ Hunt for hide-outs. Early spring is the optimum time for a blitz while the slugs and snails are still clustered together. Stacks or groups of pots, or cracks and crevices in walls, often provide a breeding ground. Tall grass around a veg bed offers easy refuge, so cut it short.

❀ Try not to water your plot at night as the extra moisture makes it easier to slime around.

❀ The many teeth of slugs and snails make swift work of young, soft plants. Try to raise plants to a decent size before hardening them off and planting outdoors. Grow spares to replace any losses.

❀ Create a physical barrier around vulnerable plants. One option is to sprinkle a circle of rough organic material around the plant, such as grit, sand, coffee grounds, finely crushed egg shells or similar. You can apply it when sowing seed or planting out seedlings or mature plants. Frequently check on the barriers and top up if necessary.

❀ Alternatively, place corrugated rings around seedlings and small plants. You can make these from recycled plastic mineral-water bottles: cut off the bottom and then remove the lid, replacing it with a piece of kitchen J-cloth or similar for ventilation, secured with an elastic band. Slot this

A circle of grit or similar rough organic material
will help protect plants from slugs and snails

over the plant, pushing it into the soil to prevent it from getting blown over by the wind. Bottles that are ridged, not smooth, work best. You can also buy similar products marketed as 'slug collars'.

❀ A barrier of copper is an effective deterrent. Slugs and snails get a small electric shock when they attempt to cross it. You can buy rolls of copper tape to staple or stick around the edge of containers or raised beds.

❀ Try 'slug pubs' in open ground. Bury empty jars or yoghurt pots, keeping the rim 2cm above ground level. (This is to stop friendly insects from falling in.) Slosh some beer (dark ale is best) into the pots – the yeast and sugars attract the slugs. Replace the liquid every few days, disposing of the molluscs.

❀ Nematodes are a modern and effective option, but pricey. These microscopic worms are natural predators that attack and kill slugs, although they are not as effective on snails. Buy them online, then mix with water to apply every six weeks or so. Note that you must water the soil first and night-time temperatures need to be above 5°C

❀ Organic slug pellets, containing ferric phosphate, are also widely available and work well. You may also find pellets made from aluminum sulphate or sheep's wool. Beware of harm to other wildlife, however: one tactic is to place the pellets under a lettuce leaf or similar to shield them from birds. Avoid non-organic pellets made from metaldehyde.

Birds

Symptoms: stripped leaves; eaten fruits, such as strawberries and redcurrants.

Some birds, notably wood pigeons, love to eat fruit buds and fruit. Pigeons will also strip the leaves of plants, especially those in the brassica family such as kales and cabbages.

❀ Use thick netting to protect fruit bushes when the fruit is starting to ripen. You can drape it over the plants or support it with a framework of

canes. Weigh down the netting at ground level. Alternatively, build or buy a fruit cage.

✿ Make your own scarecrow. Other approaches include stringing up old compact disks, which glint in the sun as a visual deterrent.

✿ Push bamboo canes into the ground and then weave in a web of fine cotton to create a physical barrier around exposed plants. Birds will then struggle to settle and feed.

Aphids

Symptoms: stunted or distorted leaves; sticky patches or spots of black mould on leaves; wilted plants.

Of the many species of these tiny insects, blackfly and greenfly are the most notorious. Aphids can reproduce asexually, without the need for mating, so the population can grow at bewildering speed – often doubling in less than a week. For this reason, it is particularly vital to keep populations down to stop attacks from escalating.

Aphids puncture the leaves to feed on the sap, which impairs the plant's growth, often causing stunted or distorted foliage. Severe infestations cause the plant to collapse. Aphids excrete a sticky, sugary substance called honeydew, which sticks to the leaves and then encourages the growth of moulds. Aphids can also spread viruses. Large populations may be visible to the naked eye. Check for the insects on the underside of leaves.

✿ Inspect regularly and keep numbers down. Squash with your fingers or blast off with a hose. Snip off and dispose of heavily affected bits of plants.

✿ Don't overfeed plants as this encourages soft growth that is tempting to the insects.

✿ Mix up your plantings to confuse and disperse the aphids, avoiding regimented rows of the same crops.

✿ Make a dilute mix of water and washing-up liquid – no more than one drop per litre of water, and spray over affected leaves. Organic soft soaps are also sold for this purpose.

✿ Consider growing decoy, sacrificial crops such as

A woven willow fence around a raised bed helps to deter cats

An upturned hanging basket will repel birds and squirrels

nasturtiums. Aphids will travel first to these crops, leaving other targets in relative peace.

❀ Although it may be impractical in small plots, it's good practice to encourage natural predators such as blue tits, ladybirds, spiders, parasitic wasps and the larvae of lacewings and hoverflies. If you have space, this involves providing suitable habitats and plants in a quest to balance friends and foes.

Cats

Symptoms: faeces around plants.

I love cats as pets, but my affection falters when they use my lettuce patch as their toilet. Frankly, it puts me right off my salad. Both your own and the neighbours' cats can be troublesome.

Cats prefer to defecate on bare, dry soil that they can easily dig, and often return to the same spot out of habit. Removing faeces swiftly can help to break their routine.

❀ Construct a barrier around tempting, bare patches: a fence of close and rigid bamboo canes is a simple option; a low, woven willow fence would be ultra-stylish. With raised beds, consider building a wooden box frame stapled with netting – fixed at the sides and removable on top. You can then step inside to tend your plants, and not worry about invading cats, birds or squirrels. Unused hanging baskets, placed upside down, can also protect individual plants.

❀ The odour of the scaredy-cat plant (*Plectranthus caninus/Coleus canina*) and the curry plant (*Helichrysum italicum*) are reputed to deter our feline foes.

❀ You can buy ultrasonic repellent devices and motion-activated water sprays, but they are expensive and I have heard mixed reviews.

Squirrels

Symptoms: uprooted plants and bulbs; holes dug in container compost.

Another destructive urban terror, squirrels often dig holes in the soil or compost, uprooting seeds, seedlings and bulbs. The only option is to cover the area with wire chicken mesh or netting, or to cover pots with upturned hanging baskets.

Red spider mite

Symptoms: pale-speckled and damaged leaves which may turn yellow or brown or develop pale yellow spots.

These mites can be a problem with indoor plants, and thrive in a dry atmosphere. They are not always red, and may be yellowy green. Heavy infestations can kill a plant. Use a magnifying glass to look for tiny insects and fine webbing on the underside of leaves. Sometimes you inadvertently import these mites when you buy or are given plants from elsewhere.

* ❀ Mist your plants with water to boost humidity levels.
* ❀ With serious infestations, you can buy biological controls such as predatory mites. These are most suitable for a greenhouse or other large indoor spaces.

Whitefly

Symptoms: tiny, white insects on leaves; sticky patches and spots of black mould on leaves; wilted plants.

An indoor pest that thrives in the warmer conditions of a windowsill or greenhouse. The minute white flies are often found on herbs such as indoor-grown basil. Like aphids, they also suck on the sap of leaves. They will fly up in a snowy mass when you shake the plant.

* ❀ Remove or squash the insects to keep the population down.
* ❀ Inspect the underside of leaves and destroy any eggs or larvae.
* ❀ Snip off and destroy any affected leaves.

Mildews

Mildews is the name given to a large group of diseases created by fungal spores in the air, many of which are actually unrelated. Powdery and downy mildew are the most common.

Powdery mildew *Symptoms: white or pale grey, dusty coating on leaves.*

Powdery mildew occurs in dry conditions. Plants are more vulnerable when stressed by irregular watering. Squashes and courgettes are particularly susceptible – it is almost inevitable towards the end of their growing season. Peas, currants, strawberries and gooseberries are also frequent victims.

* ❀ Avoid crowding plants together.
* ❀ Snip out congested leaves on individual plants to promote air circulation.
* ❀ Water to the soil around the base of plants, rather than splashing water over the leaves.
* ❀ Mulch to preserve moisture in the soil or compost: water well, then add a thick layer of organic material such as garden compost or bark chips around the base of plants.
* ❀ Swiftly dispose of affected parts of plants.

Downy mildew *Symptoms: discoloration, often yellow patches on the top of leaves; furry and fuzzy, white moulds underneath leaves.*

This is less common than powdery mildew but more lethal, and is associated with moist, humid conditions and wet leaves. It can affect many crops including lettuces, radishes and peas.

* ❀ Avoid overwatering and apply water to the soil, not the leaves.
* ❀ Try to water in the morning to decrease overnight humidity.

A pond can be successfully created in large containers, such as this salvaged bath tub

GREEN GARDENING

Unlike most things in city life, gardening does not guzzle your cash. Plants appreciate our time and attention, not the money we spend. So the process of growing plants helps to snap us out of the everyday cycle of consumerism and live with a lighter touch.

When I first started gardening, I confess that I treated it like any another hobby and a fine excuse to shop. I'd nip down to the garden centre, whip out the credit card, then return home for a whirl around my plot, leaving a trail of compost bags and plastic pots in my wake.

But now my outlook has changed. Admittedly, there are a few excellent garden centres, but I find the lacklustre examples rather depressing: bored staff sell low-quality garden tat with hefty mark-ups; trucks deliver chemically doused plants; and mountains of packaging pile up, out of view.

It's much more satisfying, I think, to buy as little as possible for your plot. Swapping and recycling can reduce outputs to a bare minimum and it's a great pleasure to re-learn rusty skills, such as seed saving. The food that we harvest also has no packaging, zero food miles and cuts down on waste, as we can pick exactly the amount that we need.

Organic gardening

There has been a long-running debate around the virtues of organic food and farming. No doubt you already have your own opinion, which guides how you shop for food. On your plot, the decision is more simple: are you happy using chemicals on your plants or not?

A non-organic approach involves buying chemical products to feed your plants and to tackle pests and diseases. If they are applied correctly, the results can be excellent, with high yields and healthy plants. But there are various down sides: the manufacturing process causes significant harm to the environment; transportation and packaging add to this impact; and the misleading appeal of these chemicals as a quick fix undermines a more balanced and long-term approach to gardening.

The organic ethos has a wider perspective and aims to improve the health of our soil, plants, wildlife and the environment. For the urban gardener, one key difference is that we ideally need to recycle kitchen scraps and other green waste to make a compost to feed our plants. You could use a wormery (see overleaf), which is ideal for small spaces, or a compost bin. There is also a wide range of other organic plant foods that you can make or buy.

Make your choice and then stick to it – a hodgepodge of the two approaches will cause a clash. For example, it's not a good idea to use organic feeds on your tomatoes then switch to a chemical product when you've run out. It's like gorging on fast food after a lifetime of healthy eating.

I grow organically. To me, it just makes total sense. Do my crops taste better? I think they do, but this issue is a red herring – it's the broader impact on our environment that's most important. I can't always buy organic food, but it's definitely how I garden.

Wildlife and biodiversity

Urban gardens are sometimes created from scratch – on a balcony or rooftop, for example. Others, such as back gardens, are already on the map for the abundant wildlife that quietly inhabits and moves around our cities.

As gardeners, we want to encourage as much life as possible onto our plots. After all, why admire only our plants? Nature offers a larger cast of marvels. Ladybirds, song birds, honey bees and hoverflies are just some of the creatures we might want to see. They also play a valuable role on our plots, often by pollinating plants or feeding on pests that will also pay us a visit.

There are many strategies for attracting wildlife, and whole books are written on the subject – I do not claim to provide all the answers here. But, in essence, we need to give them reasons to visit or set up home. Remember that wildlife likes it messy. Neat and tidy gardening – think straight rows and fussy lawns – is not their scene. So try to leave unkempt patches where they can hide: it could be a gap between the trellis and patio wall, a pile of leaves or logs, a patch of nettles or an uncovered compost heap.

Also aim to mix it up, and grow many different plants. To attract insects and birds you ideally want to offer flowers throughout the growing season, in a range of colours, shapes and textures. Berries provide excellent food for birds. Leave plants to run to seed, too, rather than tidying them away, as they are a food source for birds and a refuge for hibernating insects.

For the birds, position feeders off the ground so that they will feel safe from cats. A bird bath can be as simple as a plant saucer or a bowl with shallow sides. You can make or buy squirrel-proof bird feeders, and models that stick to windows with a sucker pad are ideal for high-rise flats.

Saving water

Water is a precious resource, so keep use to a minimum. To cut down on the frequency of your watering, always give plants a really good soak to the roots, not the leaves (see page 16). Avoid watering during the hottest part of the day to reduce evaporation from the soil or compost.

Mulching is another brilliant way to reduce water loss, both in containers and on open ground – water the plants first, then apply a thick layer of mulch around the base (see page 174).

If you have space on your outdoor plot, consider installing a water butt. This should be connected to the downpipe of a building to collect and store rainwater.

Slimline versions are available for balconies and smaller spots. This rainwater is ideal for watering all established plants. (Note, however, that tap water is recommended for germinating seeds and watering seedlings, as it is sterile.)

Vermicompost

I'm convinced that worm farms are the way forward for the urban gardener with limited space. You can easily fit a wormery on your balcony, patio or even indoors in a garage or shed. Once established, the worms can help to recycle around a fifth of a kilo of food waste per day.

Worms provide an invaluable crop – their vermicompost. Rich in microbes and nutrients, this natural compost is extremely useful for feeding plants and container growing. It is the same substance as the worm casts excreted by worms in soil. For me, it's one of the most precious harvests on my plot.

There is a wide range of wormeries available online or from your local council. You can also make your own. Suppliers typically send the worms in the post and a new wormery will take around six months to get going.

The basic composting process is the same as for a garden compost bin: you need a mixture of roughly seven parts nitrogen-rich 'green' waste, such as kitchen scraps, to three parts carbon-rich 'brown' waste, such as torn brown cardboard or egg boxes. As it decays, the worms help to break it down, passing the organic matter through their bodies and transforming it into a superior compost.

Here are some ideas for how to use your vermicompost:

❀ When preparing a compost mix for pots and containers, incorporate a few handfuls of vermicompost.

❀ To make a 'tea' to feed your plants, steep one part vermicompost, wrapped in a piece of muslin, horticultural fleece or similar, in five parts water. Shake the container a few times, then leave to stand for ten minutes or longer. Use this as a liquid feed for your plants.

oxygen and mixes the contents. The compost heats up then cools down. Addition turnings will further accelerate the process. The end product will be ready in around six months.

Whichever method you choose, always add your ingredients in thin layers. Scrunched-up brown cardboard is a handy way to introduce air pockets to the mix. Avoid adding any clippings or prunings that are thicker than a pencil.

Garden compost has multiple uses on the plot, including as a soil improver, nutritious mulch or as an ingredient in compost mixes for containers. I like to spread mine in a thick layer on my vegetable beds in early spring. The worms then drag it down into the soil.

❋ Spread a layer of vermicompost around the base of established plants. When it rains or you water the plant, the nutrients will be washed down to the roots.

❋ Add a sprinkle of vermicompost to the drill or furrow when sowing seeds.

Garden compost

If you have a garden or allotment, compost bins or compost heaps are brilliant for larger volumes of organic material. This method relies on micro-organisms such as bacteria and fungi, rather than worms. The laziest method is to cold compost – just bung in the ingredients and wait. This takes a long time, however, often a year or more.

The quicker but more laborious method is to aim for a hot compost. This requires introducing more air so that a different set of more efficient micro-organisms accelerates the process – they require oxygen to function and reproduce. To make hot compost, it's best to have two compost bins or heaps: when the first is full, you can use a garden fork to turn the ingredients into the second, which introduces more

POTS & OTHER CONTAINERS

Urban gardeners are the experts. After all, pots and containers are often our only option, especially on balconies, windowsills, window ledges and rooftops. Once we master the basics, there are some distinct advantages to this method of growing plants. Containers are moveable mini gardens that allow us to give plants the specific conditions and care that they need.

It's helpful to consider container gardening as a specialised set of skills, distinct from growing direct in the open ground. The relationship between plant and gardener is quite different, as containerised plants depend almost entirely on us for their water, food and care. Garden plants, in contrast, are far more self-sufficient. To be successful we therefore need to tune into what's going on inside the pots themselves, hidden from view

Appearance

Aesthetics matter – plants and their pots should lift the spirits, especially if you look at them every day. For years, I had an ugly hodgepodge of containers on my kitchen windowsill. But now I reserve this prime spot for my most handsome terracotta pots and recycled containers.

The first consideration is the appearance of the pots and containers themselves. Therea are also lots of tricks for disguising them, if required. Cascading plants such as bush tomatoes, trailing nasturtiums or begonias are handy for flowing over the sides. You could also slot less appealing plastic pots inside attractive terracotta pots, which also provides the best qualities of both materials – the plastic retains moisture while the terracotta offers insulation. For groups of containers, use your prettiest specimens to shield the more unsightly.

Size and shape

This is a type of matchmaking: either we want to grow a particular plant and are looking for a container of suitable size; or we've already got the container and need to choose the right plant.

It helps to imagine the plant when fully grown: its size, shape and growth habit. Most varieties of carrot, for example, will struggle in a shallow window box because they have long, slender roots; lettuces, on the other hand, require less depth so would be a better choice.

Note that the overall volume of a pot or container is just as important as its depth, so the diameter is also vital. Roots spread sideways as well as downwards, often further than we think, so it's generally wise to choose the biggest container that is practical. This will also cut down on watering, as the compost will hold more moisture.

Length of stay is another factor. A tomato seedling is best grown in a small pot but is soon moved to something larger. A gooseberry bush, however, will perhaps spend several years in the same pot so you should choose something large and durable to allow the roots to spread. Bear in mind then that it will be far more heavy and tricky to move around.

Finally, also check that any container is well balanced and won't easily tip over: a large plant in a small pot will be top-heavy, for example; containers with a wide rim and narrow base are likely to be more wobbly.

The blue-tray technique

This is my favourite system for growing a steady supply of herbs, salad leaves and microgreens, the tiny, young leaves that are a favourite with chefs. It's quick and simple, costs next to nothing and fits perfectly on my rooftop.

The containers are recycled blue plastic vegetable trays, often used for storing mushrooms and other produce. They are lightweight, a perfect size and easy to scavenge, being frequently thrown out by supermarkets, grocers and catering businesses.

I have a dozen or so trays in a row, filled with compost, and rotate them regularly: at one end are the older plants, much-harvested and nearly finished; at the other, trays that have been recently sowed.

The method:

1 Line each tray to prevent the compost from falling out and to retain moisture. Cut a sheet of any plastic, such as a bin bag or similar, to fit inside the tray. You could also use a water-permeable fabric, such as those sold in garden centres for suppressing weeds.

2 Punch or cut a dozen drainage holes in the bottom of the lining, evenly distributed and with a diameter of at least 1cm.

3 Fill each tray with multipurpose, garden or municipal compost. As the crops are fast-growing, most will do the trick. If you have vermicompost available (see page 168), mix in a few handfuls.

4 Sow a batch of seed directly into the compost, sowing the whole tray in one go. For example, sow a tray with coriander seed or a mix of mustard varieties.

5 While the seed germinates, it's helpful to slide the tray into a plastic bag or similar as this slows down evaporation and saves on watering. Check each day and remove the bag as soon as there are signs of germination.

Pots and other containers are made with a variety
of materials, each with benefits and drawbacks, as
indicated below:

MATERIAL	ADVANTAGES	DISADVANTAGES
Plastic	Inexpensive. Available in all shapes and sizes. Light, easy to move. Withstands extremes of weather. Non-porous, retains water well.	Poor insulation to extreme temperatures; roots can freeze or sweat – either is damaging to the plant. Can become brittle from exposure to light, time and wear; look out for UV-treated plastics.
Terracotta	Better insulation, provides a more stable temperature for soil or compost. Weight provides stability. Porous, so hard to overwater. Available in all shapes and sizes. Available hand- and machine-made. Glazed terracotta retains water better than unglazed.	Can crack. Unglazed terracotta is porous, so requires more watering; lining with a sheet of thick plastic will help. Not all terracotta is frost-resistant; check. Old pots can retain residues of undesirable mineral salts, so soak and wash before use.
Hardwood	Long-lasting.	Some hardwoods are from non-sustainable sources; avoid if in doubt.
Softwood	Less expensive than hardwood. Lightweight.	Short life – rots easily. Pressure-treated softwood lasts longer, but make sure it has not been treated with a preparation that includes arsenic.
Metal	Modern aesthetic.	Susceptible to extremes of temperature.
Galvanised metal	Does not rust as readily as some other metals.	Industrial look doesn't suit all settings.
Stone	Stable, hard to knock over. Long-lasting. Attractive.	Expensive. Heavy.
Concrete	Inexpensive. Can effectively replicate more expensive materials.	Can look unattractive – may need disguising.
Fibreglass	Can resemble more expensive materials. Comes in a wide range of colours. Lightweight.	Can break easily.

Drainage

Decent drainage is absolutely vital because water needs to flow easily through the compost mix. If drainage is poor, plants' roots can become waterlogged and starved of oxygen. They slowly drown and cease to function, severely affecting plant growth.

When buying pots, check that they already have drainage holes. They may also have ridges on the bottom to raise the holes off the ground, allowing water to drain away easily. With recycled or improvised containers, you may well have to add drainage holes yourself – they should have a minimum diameter of 1cm, spaced roughly 5cm apart. You can also raise containers off the ground by using pot feet, wooden batons, tiles or similar. Saucers can be placed underneath containers if you want to collect the water – for example, if growing indoors.

You may have come across the technique of filling the bottom of the container with a layer of material to help with drainage, such as terracotta shards, stones, pebbles, gravel or small chunks of broken-up polystyrene. This will do no harm, except by reducing soil volume, but a much more vital consideration is that the compost mix itself must be free-draining. Decent shop-bought composts generally offer adequate drainage, but if in doubt, or if you are mixing your own composts, add handfuls of grit, horticultural sharp sand or similar to make sure.

Watering

Containers dry out quickly, so keep a close eye. In hot weather they may well need daily watering. To judge if they are thirsty, dab your finger into the compost to feel for moisture. Try picking up a well-watered pot to hone your instinct for its weight when soaked.

If necessary, you can stand containers in saucers or trays of water so that the compost and roots can draw up water when needed. You can buy or make self-watering containers too – there are many plans online. Another option is to buy an automatic irrigation system, which allows you to leave your plants for days at a time.

The compost mix

Choosing the right compost can be confusing. Shops and garden centres offer a huge choice. The most prevalent are 'multipurpose' composts, but you will also find specialised mixes designed for seed sowing, rooting cuttings and potting on plants.

Some products are marketed as 'peat free' or with reduced levels of peat. Peat is an organic material with excellent qualities for raising plants, excavated in vast quantities to blend into commerical compost mixes. It is, however, a finite and unsustainable resource, so is best avoided. Peat substitutes include coir, the fibre from coconut husks, wood fibre and green waste.

Every compost product contains a different mix of ingredients. The key distinction, however, is between composts with no soil, such as multipurpose ones, and soil-based composts.

Most multipurpose composts are blended from organic matter – bits of plant material. They are light, in both weight and texture, and dry out relatively quickly, especially in containers. The product has been sterilised to be free from pathogens and viable weed seed. Most include chemical or organic fertilisers for added nutrients. These composts tend to contain peat or coir, and they are most suited to short-term plantings.

The second main type of composts is soil-based and includes a proportion of loam, a type of soil. These are much heavier in weight because soil includes inorganic matter, such as tiny particles of rocks. Soil-based composts are much better at retaining moisture and nutrients, and are best suited to long-term plantings. They can also include peat.

As a rule of thumb, aim to create a compost mix to suit your container and plant. For example, a large hanging basket may be too heavy if filled only with a soil-based compost. You could lighten the mix by adding half the volume of a peat-free multipurpose, so that you get the best of both.

As you become more confident, start blending your own composts – like mixing ingredients for a cake. There's a wide range of possible ingredients, each with useful properties, as shown in the table opposite.

Feeding

Plants in containers need regular feeding during the growing season, as the nutrients in shop-bought compost are typically depleted after six to eight weeks. (For more information on feeds and fertilisers, see page 17).

In general, be wary of adding dry fertilisers or manures to containers, as these are highly concentrated and can scorch roots trapped in a pot. A better option is to use liquid feeds and consider adding a slow-release fertiliser when you plant up a container, as these are designed to release their nutrients much more gradually.

Mulching

Mulching containers cuts down on watering. A mulch is a layer of material that you spread thickly on top of compost or soil to reduce evaporation. It also suppresses weeds, although these are less of a problem in containers than in the open ground. Water the container first, then apply a thick layer of mulch, at least 3cm deep, for best effect.

You can use many materials. Organic options include bark chippings and vermicompost (see page 168). Gravel, grit, stones and shells will also do the trick. Living mulches are an option too – for example, wild strawberries planted around the base of a fruit bush. In my school garden, our containerised apple trees are underplanted with a riot of nasturtiums.

Top-dressing and potting up

To give them a new lease of life, it's a good idea to top-dress plants that have been in the same container for many months. In spring, or as required, scrape off any loose compost from the top layer of the pot and replace with fresh compost. Potting up involves systematically moving plants into slightly larger pots as their root systems expand.

MATERIAL	ADVANTAGES	DISADVANTAGES	NOTES AND USES
Multipurpose compost	Cheaper than specialist mixes. Easily available. Sterile, no weeds. Lighter than a soil-based compost.	Varies in quality. Dries out quickly. Nutrients last around six weeks. Often contains peat.	Suitable for many purposes. Not suitable for containers that dry out quickly, such as hanging baskets. Be careful when sowing seeds, as the compost may be higher in nutrients than is ideal, causing seedlings to grow too fast. Often helpful to add horticultural sharp sand to improve drainage.
Homemade garden compost	Free. Sustainable. No need to transport. Decent but variable nutrient levels.	Can harbour weed seeds. Often coarse – may need sieving. Time-consuming to make. Not ideal for seed sowing.	Can be used in compost mixes or as a mulch. Good for revitalising tired compost mixes.
Council/ municipal compost	Relatively cheap. Sustainable. Light in texture.	Low in nutrients. Varies in quality. Dries out quickly. Provenance sometimes uncertain. Coarse – will need sieving. Not ideal for seed sowing.	Councils sometimes use household green waste to make their own municipal compost. Often marketed as a soil conditioner for improving soil structure, but provides few nutrients. May be better used as a mulch. For use in containers, add slow-release plant food or mix with garden compost to add nutrients.
Coir	Seen as a sustainable alternative to peat, although transporting creates some emissions. Low in nutrients, which is useful for seed sowing. Lightweight.	Typically not suitable for using on its own – best as part of a compost mix. Germination often less satisfactory compared to peat-based composts.	Fibrous material from coconut husks. Good for bulking out compost mixes. Also available in fine grade, which is useful for seed sowing.
Vermiculite	Sterile. Soaks up three to four times its volume in water. Retains nutrients where they are present.	Can trap too much water. Unsightly – can linger in soil. Issues over sustainability. Does not last as long as perlite.	Alumino-silicate clay mineral, mined and heated to expand the particles. Fine grade vermiculite is useful sprinkled over fine seeds when sowing, as it retains moisture. Professional growers often include vermiculite in compost mixes for plug plants. Good for raising seedlings, which are vulnerable to lack of moisture.
Perlite	Very light – ideal for compost mix for lightweight containers. Enhances drainage and aeration; lighter than sand. Neutral pH. Sterile. Does not rot. Lasts longer than vermiculite.	Relatively expensive. Be wary of inhaling fine perlite dust; best to dampen down before working with it. Issues over sustainability.	Silicon-rich volcanic rock heated to approximately 1,000°C to pop; lots of open pores. Used mainly for aeration and opening up mixes. Also useful in lightweight and cutting compost mixes.
Horticultural sand	Provides drainage to compost mixes and improves moisture retention. Also contains silica, a mineral compound used by plants in photosynthesis.	Far more expensive than builders' sand. Heavy.	Check it is not beach sand, which contains salt; horticultural grade is often mined from rivers.
Grit/gravel	Provides drainage to mixes. Provides trace minerals.	Heavy.	Use only horticultural or potting grit/gravel, not builders' aggregates. Available in various grades.

SAVING SEED & TAKING CUTTINGS

Of all my addictions and vices, online seed shopping seems the most harmless. It's a relatively cheap method of instant gratification, with the extra promise of reward in the months ahead.

But saving your own seed is much more satisfying and often surprisingly easy. The process is the last piece in the grow-your-own jigsaw — the final stage to master in the plant's life cycle, from birth to death. It's an ancient skill that we should all rediscover.

The seed we gather is free and often abundant — perhaps a thousand from one saved lettuce, for example, so you can swap or donate any surplus. With some plants, you also experience a spectacle that's missed when we harvest them earlier in their lifespan. Carrot flowers, for instance, shoot up only in their second year and are stunning to behold.

However, there are various practical considerations in the city. The main issue is lack of space. We want to save seed from our favourite varieties of plants in order to grow them again, but some can cross-pollinate with others growing nearby, muddling up their genetic information. Courgettes and squashes are a good example, as they are pollinated by bees and other insects that flit from flower to flower, travelling over a wide area. In the city, we don't have the space to isolate our plants so seed saving becomes problematic. Other plants, such as carrots and beetroot, take two years to bear seed, which can put pressure on your limited space and patience.

So focus your efforts on the easiest crops at first, like coriander, peas, nasturtiums, tomatoes and lettuce. These plants often pollinate themselves, as their male and female reproductive structures exist together within each flower. The specific method for saving seed for each plant is included with their individual entries in this book, but here are a few guiding principles.

❀ Don't save seed from F1 hybrids. These are plants produced by a modern selective breeding process. These hybrids are more prevalent in certain high-value crops, such as tomatoes. The plants themselves are of high quality. But if you saved and planted their seed, this next generation would not be identical to the parent. If in doubt, check your seed packet or plant label as it will clearly state 'F1' or 'hybrid'. If it does not include these words, presume it is open-pollinated and suitable for seed saving.

❀ Some plants require a long growing season in order to produce ripe seed. If you plant lettuces in early spring, for example, they stand a good chance of doing so, but mid-summer plantings will be too late.

❀ Select and reserve the strongest and most healthy specimens for saving seed. (You can harvest any others as usual.) You are aiming to preserve the best varieties with the most desirable characteristics. For instance, choose a variety of coriander which is slow to bolt (run to seed) or an open-pollinated tomato which ripens easily outdoors.

❀ Allow the seed to ripen fully on the plant. This often involves waiting for a few extra weeks past the stage at which you would normally harvest the plant to eat. With peas, for example, you want the pods to dry and wrinkle on the vine. Coriander has to flower, then its green seed will dry and mature on the plant.

❀ Some plants will happily self-seed. This means that they naturally drop their seed into the soil where they are growing, so that you get a new batch of plants popping up. Nasturtiums and chervil

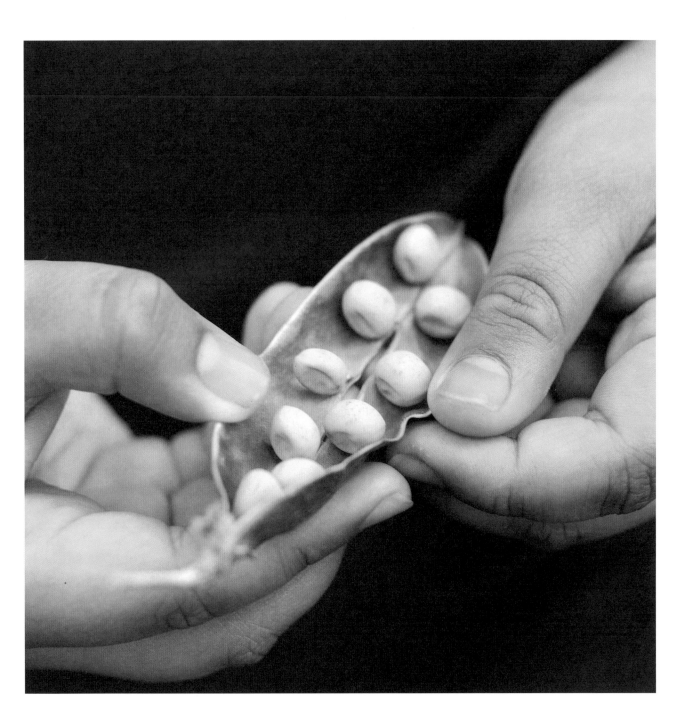

are fine examples. This habit is very handy if you want to establish a patch of a particular plant, but obviously you will need to save some seed if you want to grow it elsewhere.

❋ Dodgy weather can make seed saving difficult. You want to harvest dry and ripe seed, so persistent periods of rain can spoil your plans. You may need to uproot the whole plant and hang it upside down instead, somewhere dry.

Drying and storing seed

It is best to dry seed further indoors before you store it, as thoroughly dried seed has a longer lifespan. Choose a warm spot out of direct sun. Spread out the seed on a sheet of paper, and, if practical, turn it every day until completely dry. The duration will depend on the seed – roughly three days if it was almost dry when you saved it, to a week or more for wetter seeds.

Transfer your seed to an envelope or paper wrap and label with the date and the plant variety. Store in an airtight plastic tub or jar in the fridge as low temperature extends lifespan. Ideally include a pouch of silica gel to reduce humidity. (These are the sachets retailers include with electrical goods, new trainers and other products to keep them dry. Do not, however, buy or use the 'indicating' type of silica gels, which change colour and are possibly harmful to health.)

Before sowing, take the seeds out of the fridge and their container at least a few hours (preferably a day) in advance, so that they can return to ambient temperature. Remember that seeds are living things – we store them in a state of dormancy, which is broken when we supply the right degree of heat, moisture and darkness (for most edible plants). The viable lifespan of saved seed varies widely between crops. It's best to use carrot seed within three years, for example, but tomatoes will easily last for double that period. In general, try to use seed quickly, and, if in doubt, sow a few seeds first to test if they will happily germinate.

Cuttings

Cuttings are another method for raising new plants. You slice sections from the mother plant to grow on as new, genetically identical plants. There are many types of cutting, but two are most useful on our plots:

Semi-ripe cuttings

Suitable for: perennial herbs such as mint, thyme and lemon verbena, plus many other plants.

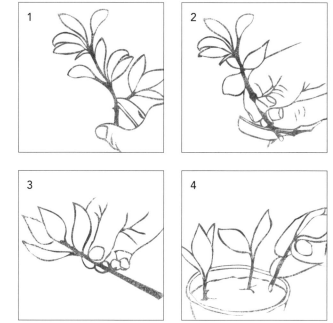

Take these cuttings from mid- to late summer, ideally in the morning. (Note that you can also take cuttings earlier in the season from younger growth – these are termed 'softwood' cuttings but follow the same basic procedure.)

❋ Choose new growth on the plant that is healthy, vigorous and non-flowering. Bend the tip of the stem between your fingers – you want a section that is soft and bendy at the top, becoming more woody and inflexible at the base.

❋ Using sharp secateurs or a knife, snip off a section around 10–20cm long. There is no prescriptive length, as plants differ widely – aim for at least four sets of leaves. Make your cut just above a leaf node on the mother plant, which is the junction where the leaves meet the stem (fig.1).

🌸 Holding the cutting in one hand, trim the stem to just below a leaf node discarding the small section you have removed (fig.2).

🌸 Strip off the leaves from the lower two thirds of the cutting (fig.3) and also remove any very soft growth at the tip. If the remaining leaves on the cutting are large, cut these in half to reduce water loss.

🌸 Fill a clean pot with a compost mix designed for cuttings. You can buy specialised cutting mixes, or make your own by mixing potting or multipurpose compost with horticultural sharp sand or grit to improve drainage. Aim for a ratio of around 6:4.

🌸 Use a pencil or dibber to make a hole in the compost, then insert the cutting. The lowest leaves should be just above compost level. Firm the compost around the cutting. You can plant several cuttings in the same pot, but make sure that the leaves do not touch (fig.4).

🌸 Water the compost well, allow to drain, and then cover the container to boost humidity. You could, for example, use a clear polythene bag, sinking canes or wire into the pot to create a supporting framework, or use a transparent plastic bottle with the bottom cut off.

🌸 Place the pot out of direct sunlight and check it every week, taking care that the cuttings do not dry out. They will take at least a month to root.

🌸 Once they have rooted, remove any cover, transfer each cutting to an individual pot and grow them on. Once they are well established, harden them off before planting outdoors.

Harwood cuttings

Suitable for: gooseberries, currants.

These cuttings are taken from autumn to mid-winter, once the leaves have fallen.

🌸 Using sharp secateurs, cut a healthy section of this year's growth around 30cm long.

🌸 Snip off the soft growth at the tip, just above a bud – use a slanted cut, sloping away from the bud (fig.5). This is to prevent any rainwater from damaging the bud and also to remind you which end is the top of the cutting.

🌸 Make a straight cut at the base of the cutting, just below a bud (fig.6).

🌸 To plant the cuttings, choose a sheltered spot outdoors, away from direct sun. You have two options: if you have space, use a spade to create a slit trench in the soil (fig.7) and incorporate some horticultural sharp sand or grit, if needed, to improve drainage; to root cuttings in a deep pot or container, fill with a compost mix designed for cuttings, as for semi-ripe cuttings. For both methods, plant the cutting so that it is two-thirds below ground level.

🌸 Water well and firm the soil or compost.

🌸 Leave the cuttings over winter, checking that they do not dry out. They should root the following spring, at which point you can pot them up or leave them to grow on. They should be well established by late summer or autumn.

PRESERVING YOUR HARVEST

Rewind the centuries, and preserving food meant survival through lean times. But our daily lives have changed beyond recognition, so which techniques are still worth the bother?

Some of the older recipes for preserving are frankly tedious. Flicking through dusty cookbooks, we're instructed to boil syrups every two days for three weeks, or to stir liquors every morning for a month with a wooden spoon.

Thankfully, that's not for us any more, as we're blessed with fridges, freezers and shops stuffed with food. We now need to update the repertoire of techniques to suit our daily lives. Modern preserving is more about fun, adding extra flavour, avoiding waste and storing away treats for the months ahead.

So let's crank up our skills: be cunning with the fridge; stock up the freezer; master the art of quick pickles; and devote the very occasional lazy Sunday to slow-cooking jams and chutneys to stash or hand out to friends.

In the tips below, I offer my take on preserving techniques – a collection of the key principles. I've simmered them down to the bare essentials, with an eye for the science behind each process. In this, I must thank the writer Harold McGee, whose brilliant books, including *McGee on Food and Cooking*, have helped to demystify that which we often take for granted.

Refrigeration

The fridge is a brilliant invention, but lazy fridge culture has also fostered bad habits. A fridge works by circulating cool air around our food, ideally at 4°c, which reduces metabolic activity and microbial growth, therefore extending its edible life.

This air also has a drying effect, however, which is why it's best to wrap or seal exposed foods before refrigerating them. The low temperatures also dull flavour, so cold foods tend to taste more bland. In most cases, the flavours will revive if the food is allowed to return to room temperature. Some foods, however, are permanently damaged by incarceration in the fridge.

❋ As a rule of thumb, don't refrigerate vegetables or fruit that thrive in warmer climates. Home-grown examples include tomatoes, squashes and basil. Store these at room temperature, out of direct sunlight.

❋ To refrigerate salad leaves, most herbs and leafy vegetables, wrap first in a brown paper bag or an unsealed plastic bag. The plants will continue to respire in the fridge, producing moisture, so sealing encourages condensation and sogginess. With salad leaves and herbs, I also pop a sheet of kitchen paper into the bag to help soak up moisture.

❋ Plan ahead and allow food to return to room temperature before you eat or cook it. This also saves energy during the cooking process as it takes longer to heat chilled foods.

❋ A near-empty fridge wastes energy – try to keep it around two-thirds full.

Freezing

Good for: chillies, edible flowers, herbs, soft fruits, vegetables.
I love my freezer, and so should you. Often under-used, freezers are the easiest way to stretch the season. Low temperatures of minus 18°C and below reduce metabolic activity and microbial growth to near zero. Well-packed food can be stored for long periods with only very gradual deterioration. Not all items enjoy the freezer, but those that do emerge in fine condition.

My dream freezer is packed with the following: ready-to-cook chopped chillies and chives; ice cubes containing edible flowers; tomato sauces; herb butters; and supplies of whole gooseberries, currants and other vegetables. I also use my freezer for sensory effect: crudités are crunchier after 15 minutes in the freezer; grapes are great after a couple of hours.

❋ Freeze foods in small quantities. This makes the freezing process faster, forming smaller ice crystals in the food and minimising damage to texture.

❋ Wrap or seal food in handy portions, aiming to avoid freezer burn when the food dries out and discolours when exposed to air. Wrap larger items in at least two plastic freezer bags, smaller items in one, and squeeze out as much air as possible. Alternatively, use plastic containers or cling film. Sealing also stops food from absorbing rogue aromas. Label your produce with the contents and date, as it is easy to forget these a few months later.

* For chillies and chives, use the 'dry' ice-cube technique, with an ice-cube tray and no water. Chop them up first into convenient mini portions, scoop into ice-cube trays and freeze. (Transfer later to a freezer bag if you like.) You can use these when cooking with no need to defrost.

* For edible flowers, use the 'wet' ice-cube technique. Half fill the trays with water, add the flowers, freeze, then top up with water and freeze again. Pop them straight into drinks for a splash of colour.

* For herbs, you can freeze bunches whole but leaf texture and flavour deteriorate. Herb butters are a much better idea: mix chopped herbs into softened butter, adding sea salt and lemon juice to taste; on a sheet of greaseproof paper, roll the butter into a cylinder, twisting each end like a cracker; wrap again in cling film and freeze. Chop off portions when needed – for example, to melt over steamed vegetables or grilled meat.

* For soft fruits, freeze using the 'open-tray' technique. Freeze first in a single layer, spread out on a baking tray covered with greaseproof paper, then transfer to freezer bags or containers.

* Some produce needs blanching before freezing. This is when you briefly plunge it into boiling water, then into a bowl of iced water to halt the cooking process. The heat destroys enzymes and micro-organisms, preserving texture and prolonging storage life. I blanch only if I have a large glut to store, and don't find it necessary for some items such as chillies and chives.

* Defrost items thoroughly if appropriate, ideally in the fridge. Do not refreeze. As a rule of thumb, eat produce within six months.

Instant pickles

Good for: beetroots, cabbages, carrots, chillies, cucumbers, mouse melons, radishes and turnips.

Instant pickles take moments to make, taste great and are infinitely versatile. This technique aims to enhance flavour and texture rather than extend storage life. They typically feature crunchy vegetables, often salted first to improve texture, with an extra hit of acidity, sweetness and perhaps a few subtle spices.

This style of pickles is common in East Asian countries, especially Japan, which boasts hundreds of pickled dishes called tsekumono. But they are little used in the West. They store for up to three days in the fridge.

* Sprinkling salt over food is an ancient technique of food preparation and preservation. The salt draws out water from the food cells which alters and improves texture and flavours. It works best with produce that has a high water content, such as radishes or mouse melons, chopped first to expose their flesh to the salt. You can then wash the salt off, if desired, once it has performed its magic. Always use natural sea salt or rock salt, not table salt, as the latter includes chemical anti-caking agents. As a rule of thumb, add 2 per cent salt in proportion to the weight of the vegetables.

* Note that you can also use a salt solution to similar effect, dissolving salt in water to create a 'wet brine'. When pickling, this method is typically used for drier vegetables with a lower water content, such as cauliflowers or onions, which are often soaked overnight. Aim for a 10 per cent brine by using 50g salt to every 500ml water.

* For a Japanese-style instant pickle try a rainbow of crisp radishes with a hint of lemon (see page 55).

* For a more Western-style pickle, chop carrots into batons and sprinkle with lemon juice or wine vinegar or cider vinegar, caster sugar, salt and chopped herbs. Add other crunchy vegetables such as kohl rabi if you fancy.

* For an instant dipping sauce, pickle a chopped chilli in rice wine vinegar (see page 28).

Fridge pickles

Good for: beetroots, cabbage, carrots, cauliflowers, chillies, courgettes, cucumbers, mouse melons, radishes, winter squashes and turnips.

These are a shortcut on a traditional slow pickle and are best eaten swiftly and stored in the fridge. They are made without the precision and careful sterilisation involved in preparing a slow pickle.

Unlike instant pickles, fridge pickles involve boiling up vinegar, often with added spices and a touch of sugar, to pour over the vegetables. For firm vegetables, such as carrot or beetroot, you can pour over the liquid while still hot. This will slightly cook and soften them. You could also add the vegetables to the liquid when it's boiling if you want to cook them further. For softer vegetables, such as cucumbers or mouse melons, let the liquid cool first.

❁ Texture is all-important, so use fresh produce in its prime. It is often best to pick vegetables when they are young: for example, baby beetroot or sweet young carrots.

❁ Chop vegetables to the size you prefer. For extra crunch, salt first before adding the pickling liquid (see page 182).

❁ The basic process for preparing a pickling liquid is to bring vinegar, spices and sugar (to taste) to the boil for 2 minutes. Use whole rather than ground spices to prevent cloudiness.

❁ Experiment with different vinegars and sugars: for example, white wine vinegar or cider vinegar makes a clear pickle; malt vinegar is darker and boldly flavoured; brown muscovado sugar is more complex in taste than refined white sugar.

❁ Some recipes call for diluting the pickling liquid – for example, by adding three parts water to one part vinegar, or adding wine to the mixture for extra flavour. This mellows the sharp taste of the pickling liquid. But note that it also reduces the acidity and therefore its preservative qualities, and should never be done with pickles intended for long-term storage.

❁ For a quick cucumber or mouse melon pickle, try flavouring with dill or ginger (see page 46).

❁ Use sterilised jars if you want to store the pickles for more than a few days (see below).

Slow pickles

Good for: beetroots, carrots, chillies, courgettes, cucumbers, mouse melons, radishes and winter squashes.

Traditional slow pickles are designed for long-term storage, out of the fridge, so they require extra care with the strength of vinegar and sterilisation of the jar and pickle contents. The process for creating the pickling liquid is the same as for fridge pickles. Slow pickles will improve in flavour over time. They are best eaten after one month and will store for six months or more.

❁ As with quicker styles of pickles, salting produce first will improve texture (see page 182).

❁ Sterile jars are essential to reduce the risk of spoilage. If the jars are recycled, remove any labels first and scrupulously wash both jars and lids with soap and water. One method for sterilisation is to put them through your dishwasher's hot cycle immediately prior to use. Alternatively, place them in a pan, fill with cold water, bring to the boil for 1 minute, then allow to cool. Another method is to use the oven: wash and dry the jars, then place them in a cold oven; turn to 150°C/300°F/gas 2, leave for half an hour, then carefully remove. For the lids, scrub with soap and water, rinse, then sterilise in boiling water, as above.

❁ Vinegar reacts adversely with some metals, so only use jars with plastic-lined lids. For the same reason, use stainless-steel or enamel pans rather than copper, brass or iron. Check the acidity levels before using any speciality vinegars – they must contain at least 5 per cent acetic acid to preserve the produce effectively. Balsamic vinegar is not suitable.

❁ Pack the vegetables into warm, sterilised jars, then pour the pickling liquid right to the top in order to exclude as much air as possible. Check for air bubbles in the jars – give them a firm tap or poke in a clean skewer to pierce bubbles.

❀ Store pickles in a dark place. Once they have been opened, store in the fridge. When serving, fish out the pickles with a clean fork or tongs.

Chutneys

Good for: apples, beetroots, carrots, courgettes, gooseberries, rhubarb, tomatoes, pears, plums and many other fruits and vegetables.

Chutneys take their time – at least two hours, gently simmering to deepen flavour – so they resent a cook in a rush. Both vinegar and sugar act as preserving agents. Chutneys are best eaten after one month and will store for up to two years.

❀ Surplus is the soul of chutneys – use whatever produce is on hand and don't slavishly follow a recipe.

❀ Aim for texture, not a homogenous paste. Chop the fruit and vegetables by hand into even-shaped small chunks, cutting out blemishes or bruises.

❀ Use a heavy-based stainless-steel pan. Simmer chutneys gently, uncovered, to keep the pieces intact and stir regularly – particularly towards the end of the process, to prevent sticking and burning.

❀ As a rough guide, for each kilo of mixed fruit or vegetables add 250ml vinegar, 200g brown sugar, one chopped onion and a pinch of salt. For extra flavour, consider adding fresh ginger, chilli, sultanas or fresh horseradish. Spices such as cinnamon, cumin, cardamom, cloves and coriander seed should be tied in a muslin spice bag.

❀ The flavours mingle and develop, so taste and adjust as you go. Chutneys will mature and improve with age.

❀ Chutneys are ready when thick and viscous. To judge, scrape your spoon along the bottom of the pan – the chutney should part, revealing the metal for a couple of seconds, before coalescing.

❀ Pour the chutney into warm sterilised jars. I use

a jug and a funnel – with the bottom cut off to enlarge the hole. Fill right to the top of the jar to exclude as much air as possible. Check for air bubbles (see left). Seal with a vinegar-proof lid and store in a cool, dark place.

Jams, conserves and marmalades

Good for: currants, gooseberries and other fruit.

Jams are fruit cooked to a pulp with sugar. Conserves, on the other hand, tend to include whole fruit or chunks. Marmalades are made from citrus fruit with a rind, such as Seville oranges or grapefruits.

All rely on pectin, a natural substance in the fruit, to set. Pectin reacts with the sugar and the fruit's natural acid. This acidity varies, depending on the type of fruit – gooseberries and currants are high in pectin, for example, while strawberries are low. You can use shop-bought pectin to top up.

❀ Sterilise all jars and lids (see opposite). Either metal or plastic-lined lids are fine.

❀ Use blemish-free, slightly under-ripe fruit. Do not add ginger as this can affect the setting point.

❀ Simmer the fruit, then gradually add granulated sugar, warmed first in a baking tray in a moderate oven. Let the sugar dissolve before cranking up the heat to bring the mixture to the boil and reach setting point – the stage at which sugars and pectin have reacted sufficiently for the jam to set when it cools. You need to heat your jam to a high temperature, so gas hobs are more effective. If you have an electric hob, only make jam in small quantities.

❀ To test for setting point, first put a plate in the fridge to cool. Then place a spoonful of jam on the cooled plate. Meanwhile, take the jam off the heat. Blow on the sample to cool it down. If it forms a skin, the jam is ready. If not, turn the heat back on and cook further.

❀ Pour into warm jars, right up to the top, seal, cool and store in a dark place.

RESOURCES

General gardening

Garden Organic
gardenorganic.org.uk
A charity devoted to organic gardening.

Royal Horticultural Society
rhs.org.uk
The prestigious gardening charity in Britain.

Food growing

City Farmer
cityfarmer.info
News and resources relating to urban food production.

Kitchen Gardeners International
kitchengardeners.org
Online global community focused on food growing.

Seed suppliers

B and T World Seeds
b-and-t-world-seeds.com
Vast seed catalogue, specialising in unusual and exotic seeds.

CN Seeds
cnseeds.co.uk
Excellent range of herb seeds.

Edwin Tucker and Sons
edwintucker.com
Large catalogue of organic seed.

Evergreen Seeds
evergreeseeds.com
Californian supplier of more than 350 varieties of Asian vegetable seeds.

Jungle Seeds
jungleseeds.co.uk
Supplier of more unusual seeds, such as mouse melons.

Real Seeds
realseeds.co.uk
Open-pollinated varieties of seed and advice for seed saving.

Stormy Hall Seeds
stormy-hall-seeds.co.uk
Supplier of biodynamic seeds.

Thomas Etty
thomasetty.co.uk
Heritage seeds and bulbs.

Tozers Seeds
tozerseeds.com
Best for large quantities of seed.

Seed saving

Heritage Seed Library
gardenorganic.org.uk/hsl
Membership scheme to share traditional varieties.

Kokopelli
kokopelli-seeds.com
Based in France, supplier of open-pollinated varieties of seed.

Seed Savers Exchange
seedsavers.org
Based in USA, offering advice and selling open-pollinated varieties of seed.

Sowing New Seeds
sowingnewseeds.org.uk
Project researching exotic crops not traditionally grown in Britain.

The Seed Ambassadors Project
seedambassadors.org
Seed-saving network in USA.

Plug plants

Delfland Nurseries
organicplants.co.uk
Excellent supplier of plug plants.

Sea Spring Seeds
seaspringseeds.co.uk
Supplier of chilli plants and other vegetable seeds.

Container growing

EarthBox
earthbox.com
Supplier of well-designed self-watering containers.

The Balcony Gardener
thebalconygardener.com
Supplier of window boxes and other containers.

Vertical Veg
verticalveg.org.uk
Tips and advice from container expert Mark Ridsdill Smith.

Nurseries

Agroforestry Research Trust
agroforestry.co.uk
Supplier of unusual plants.

Blackmoor Nurseries
blackmoor.co.uk
Wide range of fruit.

Edulis
edulis.co.uk
Supplier of rare edible plants.

R. V. Roger
rvroger.co.uk
Supplier of soft fruit and other plants, with an exceptional range of gooseberries.

Victorian Violas
victorianviolas.co.uk
Specialist in violas.

Pests and diseases

Defenders
defenders.co.uk
Supplier of biological pest controls.

Nemasys
nemasysinfo.com
Supplier of nematodes, with useful information on pests.

Preserving

Just Preserving
justpreserving.co.uk
Suppliers of preserving equipment.

Lakeland
lakeland.co.uk
Suppliers of preserving equipment.

Seasoned Pioneers
seasonedpioneers.co.uk
Spice specialist.

Bees

Bee Base
nationalbeeunit.com
Information and resources from The National Bee Unit.

British Beekeepers Association
bbka.org.uk
Leading charity for amateur beekeepers.

National Bee Supplies
beekeeping.co.uk
Supplier of beekeeping equipment.

The Hive Honey Shop
thehivehoneyshop.co.uk
A shop selling a huge range of honeys and other bee products.

Chickens

Ascott
ascott-dairy.co.uk
Poultry supplies, garden tools and more.

Omlet
omlet.co.uk
Supplier of a wide range of equipment, with a lively online community.

Perfect Poultry
perfectpoultry.co.uk
Supplier of chickens, bantams and equipment.

Worms

Wiggly Wigglers
wigglywigglers.co.uk
Supplier of a wide range of wormeries and compost bins.

The Worm Research Centre
wormresearchcentre.co.uk
Useful information about the benefits of worms.

Worms Direct
wormsdirect.co.uk
Supplier of worms and wormeries.

BIBLIOGRAPHY

ANDREWS, JEAN: *Peppers: The Domesticated Capsicums*. University of Texas Press, 1995.

ANDREWS, JEAN: *The Peppers Cookbook*. University of North Texas Press, 2005.

BAYLESS, RICK and BAYLESS, DEANN GROEN: *Authentic Mexican: Regional Cooking from the Heart of Mexico*. Headline, 1989.

BOWN, DENI: *The Royal Horticultural Society Encyclopedia of Herbs and Their Uses*. Dorling Kindersley, 1995.

CHEIFITZ, PHILLIPPA: *Cooking with Chillies, Peppers and Spices*. New Holland, 1994.

COBBETT, WILLIAM: *The English Gardener*. Bloomsbury, 1998.

CUNNIGHAM, SALLY: *Asian Vegetables*. Eco-Logic Books, 2009.

DAVIDSON, ALAN: *The Oxford Companion to Food*. Oxford University Press, 2006.

DOWDING, CHARLES: *How to Grow Winter Vegetables*. Green Books, 2011.

DOWDING, CHARLES: *Salad Leaves for All Seasons*. Green Books, 2008.

GARLAND, SARAH: *The Complete Book of Herbs and Spices*. Frances Lincoln, 2004.

GARLAND, SARAH: *The Herb Garden*. Frances Lincoln, 2003.

GRIGSON, JANE: *Jane Grigson's Vegetable Book*. Penguin Books, 1998.

GUERRA, MICHAEL: *The Edible Container Garden*. Gaia Books, 2005

HELOU, ANISSA: *Modern Mezze*. Quadrille Publishing, 2008.

LARKCOM, JOY: *Grown Your Own Vegetables*. Frances Lincoln, 2002.

LARKCOM, JOY: *Oriental Vegetables*. Frances Lincoln, 2007.

LARKCOM, JOY: *The Organic Salad Garden*. Frances Lincoln, 2003.

MABEY, DAVID AND ROSE: *The Penguin Book of Jams, Pickles and Chutneys*. Penguin Books, 1988.

McFADDEN, CHRISTINE and MICHAUD, MICHAEL: *Cool Green Leaves and Red Hot Peppers*. Frances Lincoln, 1998.

McGEE, HAROLD: *McGee on Food and Cooking: An Encyclopedia of Kitchen Science, History and Culture*. Hodder and Stoughton, 2004.

RAVEN, SARAH: *Sarah Raven's Garden Cookbook*. Bloomsbury Publishing, 2007.

RAVEN, SARAH: *The Great Vegetable Plot*. BBC Books, 2011.

RODGERS, JUDY: *The Zuni Café Cookbook*. W. W. Norton and Co, 2003.

ROUND, JEREMY: *The Independent Cook*. Pan Books, 2001.

STOCKS, CHRISTOPHER: *Forgotten Fruits: The Stories Behind Britain's Traditional Fruit and Vegetables*. Windmill Books, 2009.

VAUGHAN, J. G. and GEISSLER, C. A.: *The New Oxford Book of Food Plants*. Oxford University Press, 1999.

YOUNG, PAUL A.: *Adventures with Chocolate*. Kyle Cathie, 2009.

INDEX

First published in Great Britain in 2012 by
Kyle Books, an imprint of Kyle Cathie Ltd
23 Howland Street
London, W1T 4AY
www.kylebooks.com

ISBN: 978-1-85626-986-5

Text © 2012 Tom Moggach
Photographs © 2012 Laura Hynd
Except for Tom Moggach pp.11, 12, 27, 33, 34 bottom, 54
top and middle, 79, 132, 135, 137 and 144; Sarah Cuttle
p.9: top right; Mike Lieberman p.9: bottom left; Pedro Diez
p.9: bottom right; Mark Bolton/Garden Picture Library/
Getty Images p.67; Gert Tabak The Netherlands/Garden
Picture Library/Getty Images p.71; Juliette Wade/Garden
Picture Collection/Getty Images p.80: top and p.105.
Design © 2012 Kyle Books

Tom Moggach is hereby identified as the author of this
work in accordance with Section 77 of the Copyright,
Designs and Patents Act 1988.

Editors: Judith Hannam and Catharine Robertson
Designer and illustrator: Laura Yates
Photographer: Laura Hynd
Food stylist: Lizzie Harris
Props stylist: Claudia Bryan
Production: Gemma John and Nic Jones

A Cataloguing In Publication record for this title is available
from the British Library.
Printed in China by C&C Offset Printing Limited.

Acknowledgements

Many thanks to the following people – their kind help
made the writing of this book possible:

The team at Kyle Books for their expertise and support,
Clare Hulton for her guidance, Laura Hynd for her beautiful
images, Laura Yates for her brilliant design and Lizzie Harris
for her cooking and styling.

My wife Larushka and daughter Lyra, whose love and
patience will never be forgotten.

Victoria Ennion for her horticultural wisdom (crowsfoot.
co.uk) and Talia Lash for her assistance with the text.

Mark Ridsill Smith for his friendship and support
(verticalveg.org.uk).

Sara Davies and the wonderful team at Hawkwood
(organiclea.org.uk) for their inspiration.

Capital Growth for their great work in my home city
(capitalgrowth.org).

Gardener and author Marc Diacono, whose teaching
helped me to embark on this journey (otterfarm.co.uk).

Hedvig Murray and Alex Collings from Get Growing
(getgrowing.org.uk) for sharing their Growing Club
sessions, run on behalf of Somerford and Shacklewell
Tenants and Residents Association with funding from City
and Hackney Primary Care Trust and the Learning Trust.

Kentish Town City Farm (ktcityfarm.org.uk), Camley Street
Natural Park (wildlondon.org.uk), Rhyl Primary School,
Maddalena Polletta and Pedro Diez in New York and Mike
Lieberman in Los Angeles (urbanorganicgardener.com),
who all helped with images for this book.

Victorian Violas for their specialist help and plants
(victorianviolas.co.uk).